SHORTCUT 5

317 SUCCESS QUOTES

by LINKED IN AND TOWN HALL ACHIEVER OF THE YEAR
EY NOMINEE ENTREPRENEUR OF THE YEAR
GRAND HOMAGE LYS DIVERSITY
WORLD TOP100 DOCTORS

Dr BAK NGUYEN, DMD

TO ALL THOSE LOOKING TO WALK THEIR LEGENDS AND TO IMPACT THE WORLD WITH THEIRS SUCCESSES

by Dr BAK NGUYEN

ISBN: 978-1-989536-78-0

Published by: Dr. BAK PUBLISHING COMPANY
Dr.BAK 0097

DISCLAIMER

« The general information, opinions and advice contained in this medium and/or the books, audiobooks, podcasts and publications on Dr. Bak Nguyen's (legal name Dr. Ba Khoa Nguyen) website or social media (hereinafter the "Opinions") present general information on various topics. The Opinions are intended for informational purposes only.

No information contained in the Opinions is a substitute for an expert, consultation, advice, diagnosis or professional treatment. No information contained in the Opinions is a substitute for professional advice and should not be construed as consultation or advice.

Nothing in the Opinions should be construed as professional advice related to the practice of dentistry, medical advice or any other form of advice, including legal or financial advice, professional opinion, care or diagnosis, but strictly as general information. All information from the Opinions is for informational purposes only.

Any user who disagrees with the terms of this Disclaimer should immediately cease using or referring to the Opinions. Any action by the user in connection with the information contained in the Opinions is solely at the user's discretion.

The general information contained in the Opinions is provided "as is" and without warranty of any kind, either expressed or implied. Dr. Bak Nguyen (legal name Dr. Ba Khoa Nguyen) makes every effort to ensure that the information is complete and accurate. However, there is no guarantee that the general information contained in the Opinions is always available, truthful, complete, up-to-date or relevant.

The Opinions expressed by Dr. Bak Nguyen (legal name Dr. Ba Khoa Nguyen) are personal and expressed in his own name and do not reflect the opinions of his companies, partners and other affiliates.

Dr. Bak Nguyen (legal name Dr. Ba Khoa Nguyen) also disclaims any responsibility for the content of any hyperlinks included in the Opinions.

Always seek the advice of your expert advisors, physicians or other qualified professionals with any questions you may have regarding your condition. Never disregard professional advice or delay in seeking it because of something you have read, seen or heard in the Opinions. »

ABOUT THE AUTHOR

From Canada, **Dr. BAK NGUYEN**, Nominee Ernst and Young Entrepreneur of the year, Grand Homage Lys DIVERSITY, LinkedIn & TownHall Achiever of the year and TOP 100 Doctors 2021. Dr Bak is a cosmetic dentist, CEO and founder of Mdex & Co. His company is revolutionizing the dental field. Speaker and motivator, he wrote 72 books over 36 months accumulating many world records (to be officialized). His books are covering:

- **ENTREPRENEURSHIP**
- **LEADERSHIP**
- **QUEST OF IDENTITY**
- **DENTISTRY AND MEDICINE**
- **PARENTING**
- **CHILDREN'S BOOKS**
- **PHILOSOPHY**

In 2003, he founded Mdex, a dental company upon which in 2018, he launched the most ambitious private endeavour to reform the dental industry, Canada wide. Philosopher, he has close to his heart the quest of happiness of the people surrounding him, patients and colleagues alike. In 2020, he launched an International collaborative initiative named **THE ALPHAS** to share knowledge and for Entrepreneurs and Doctors to thrive through the Greatest Pandemic and Economic depression of our time.

In 2016, he co-found with Tranie Vo, Emotive World Incorporated, a tech research company to use technology to empower happiness and sharing. U.A.X. the ultimate audio experience is the landmark project on which the team is advancing, utilizing the technics of the movie industry and the advancement in ARTIFICIAL INTELLIGENCE to save the book industry and to upgrade the continuing education space.

These projects have allowed Dr Nguyen to attract interests from the international and diplomatic community and he is now the centre of a global discussion in the wellbeing and the future of the health profession. It is in that matter that he shares his thoughts and encourages the health community to share their own stories.

"It's not worth it go through it alone! Together, we stand, alone, we fall."

Motivational speaker and serial entrepreneur, philosopher and author, from his own words, Dr Nguyen describes himself as a dentist by circumstances, an entrepreneur by nature and a communicator by passion.

He also holds recognitions from the Canadian Parliament and the Canadian Senate.

SHORTCUT 5

317 SUCCESS QUOTES

by Dr BAK NGUYEN

INTRODUCTION
BY Dr BAK NGUYEN

CONCLUSION
BY Dr BAK NGUYEN

ANNEX
GLOSSARY OF Dr. BAK's LIBRARY
Dr. BAK NGUYEN

PART 1
SUCCESS
Dr. BAK NGUYEN

PART 2
104 SUCCESS QUOTES
Dr. BAK NGUYEN

PART 3
BUSINESS
Dr. BAK NGUYEN

PART 4
136 BUSINESS QUOTES
Dr. BAK NGUYEN

PART 5
THE POWER OF QUOTES
Dr. BAK NGUYEN

PART 6
77 FAMOUS QUOTES
Dr. BAK NGUYEN

INTRODUCTION
by Dr. BAK NGUYEN

Apple Books just approved a few hours earlier the 4th volume of the **SHORTCUT** series, **CONFIDENCE**, making it available in 51 countries. This was book #096. With the 2 uncompleted titles (**COVIDCONOMICS** and **CRYPTOCONOMY**) this brings me to 6 books left to write before reaching the next world record of writing 100 books in 4 years.

I am still unsure of the outcome of this challenge since each book is unique but I and very confident. I've submitted the paperback and kindle version of **SHORTCUT volume 4, CONFIDENCE** to Amazon and it should be released as morning comes. Yes, morning.

It is 2:47 AM and I just woke up. I should be returning to bed since I have a full clinical day in a few hours, just like I had yesterday. Clinical days are intense and demanding on my concentration, it does not leave much attention left to do anything else. That said, in between my patients, I always try to make the most of each moment.

But that is not what is pushing me to write this introduction and to start, yet another book, book #097. What is pushing me this time are the numbers and the *wave of momentum*.

I was awake, surfing the web on my smartphone when I realized that Barnes and Noble just made the 3rd volume, **SHORTCUT volume 3, LEADERSHIP** available. Like each time, that was a great feeling of victory, of confidence.

Even if I am writing books at a 2-3 days interval, the completion and the release of each book is still generating the same feeling of satisfaction. That in turn, feeds me with more Confidence and keeps me in action, with all the adrenaline and hormones flowing.

So I did what was expected of me, I pulled my calculator out and divided the numbers of days left (28) by the number of books left to write (6). That gave me the odds of 4.5 days per book! That is not much, insane you will say. Well, that is much better than the odds of 3.7 days per book that I was looking at a week ago!

In the introduction of my last book, **SHORTCUT volume 4, CONFIDENCE**, the odds were at 4.43 days per book. That's maybe not much of an improvement, nonetheless, it is a step in the right direction.

I couldn't resist the temptation to immortalize the improvement of my odds and my win of 0.07 days per book on my previous odds. That's 1 hour and 41 minutes that I just gain on average per book left to write. In other words, at my current speed, that's more than the time to write a chapter per book. This is not nothing!

On the other hand, watching the **Tokyo 2020 Olympic games**, I got a glimpse of the Olympian's mindset, investing years of training to win by 0.01 seconds. 1 second at the Olympics is the difference between the podium and not even making the finals in some sports!!!

They cannot achieve such greatness by discarding each small improvement of their performance. In **SHORTCUT volume 4, CONFIDENCE**, we learnt that Confidence is growing from every single win. Moving from one win to the next is how we are building up, both momentum and confidence.

Well, 0.07 days is a huge win, especially considering the trend emerging. From an average of 3.7 days to 4.5 days per book, over a period of 10 days, that cannot be discounted. I gained 0.8 days odds writing and publishing 4 books since my return from Vancouver for the shooting and researches for **COVIDCONOMICS**.

"I can't stop now, my body won't allow it. That is what momentum will do to you."
Dr. Bak Nguyen

That's quote #2451. This introduction was very technical and yet, it shows the mechanical, psychological and physiological process behind the exploits and the mindset. Actually, the breakthrough that I just realized right at this moment is that it is no longer a mindset but it has become a reflex. And this is the next phase of evolution.

"Momentum will bring the best out of you, upgrading your mindset into reflex."
Dr. Bak Nguyen

That's quote #2452. And here comes the next volume of the series, **SHORTCUT volume 5, SUCCESS**. In the precedent volumes, we went from healing to growth, then to leadership, and then, confidence, success should be the natural next step of the journey, rising. I told you that rising is the best part of the journey, haven't I?

I realized that this could be either the introduction of the next instalment in the **SHORTCUT SERIES** or the introduction of **TIMING, TIME MANAGEMENT ON STEROIDS**. It would make sense to take a break and write about something else for a few days (TIMING).

If I listen to my mind, I would have take the diversion but my body is pushing hard and is in control right now. My hormones and instincts are pushing me toward keeping Momentum, maintaining the cap on the **SHORTCUT series**. The words wrote themselves. This is how success came as a reflex.

"A Momentum is reached the day that it is easier to move forward than to stop."
Dr. Bak Nguyen

Success is many things and can be explained by many, many factors. Luck, hard work, resilience, determination, passion, talent, training, environment, timing are all contributing factors. Amongst those, hard work, resilience, determination, passion, and training are derived from knowing who we are and knowing what we want. We covered those already.

Environment, we covered that one in **SHORTCUT volume 4, CONFIDENCE** with the presence of mentors and proteges. Only luck and timing are still left for inquiry. Well, these 2 will be the questions raised approaching the 5th volume of **SHORTCUT**, retracing the **SUCCESSES** both in business and personal growth to understand how to harness and leverage from both, **LUCK** and **TIMING**.

Don't look at me, I don't know yet. I walked the journey but I haven't had the chance to revisit my wins and successes to understand what happened and how I found leverage. You will be sharing with me these reflections in real-time in this journey.

This is **Shortcut volume 5, SUCCESS**. Welcome to the Alphas.

Dr. BAK NGUYEN

PART 1
"SUCCESS"
by Dr. BAK NGUYEN

Well, what is success? I hate this kind of chapter of what is something. That said, I believe that there are 2 kinds of successes, the ones people gave us, accomplishing a competition, successfully completing an exam, or defending your thesis. Those are the ones that we usually move forward from in our everyday life as we are moving up the ladders.

There is also the other kind of successes, those in which you know you made a difference in someone else's life. You may not receive a medal or a diploma by the end of that journey, but you know and feel that you were useful and did make a difference.

SELF-ACTUALIZATION

ESTEEM

LOVE/BELONGING

SAFETY

PHYSIOLOGICAL NEEDS

THE PYRAMID OF ABRAHAM MASLOW

I am not taking anything away from the first kind of success but if we try to match them in the Pyramid of Maslow, they will be located in the belonging level since that is the recognition of peers and of management that decided if it was a success or not.

You proved that you are good enough, even, the best, but that was still a test, a simulation, not real life. At best, you will have found great esteem but this is no purpose.

With the second kind of success, you are not looking for self-recognition nor any kind of validation, you are delivering. Only the outcome matter as your skills and sciences are needed to solve a problem. Unfortunately, this kind is the less celebrated victory, those where you are making a difference.

It often did not come with any medal or a public other than the person that you are servicing. Even if this kind of success happened on a daily basis to some, we do not make much of a deal of it, because it was on a daily basis.

We are so wrong about our perception of success. No wonder why so many are stuck in scarcity and spend their lives looking for abundance. If they only celebrate scarcity, they will never recognize abundance!

Don't be mistaken. Any success is a good success. But as you only celebrate those who come in only once in a while, the celebration will rhyme with once in a while. That is food for your spirit and confidence. Will you accept to eat just once in a while?

And what happened to someone who is hungry and is looking for food, for days? Well, he tunnels vision to see only what he can eat and what is within reach, narrowing much of the possibilities and what else Life has to offer.

Spend too much time in that stasis and that mindset will slowly grow into a reflex, deeply integrated with our perception of life. Stuck in that, even if you stand on abundance, you will not recognize it.

To come back at the 2 kinds of successes, if your successes are only celebrated with the approval of the others, you are giving the control of your feeding (spirit) to the crowd and to **management**.

They will be in control of your growth and satisfaction, not you. They will be in control of its pace and frequency, even if you gave it your best, you are not in control. This is why, even if you have a huge boost of esteem and of confidence, those were conditional.

Serving others is our way to find our purpose and esteem, on our own terms. So are we all heroes and champions, making a difference on a daily basis? Well, here comes the **trap of Conformity**.

We were doing that based on the licenses and competences that Society granted us. Since Society does not celebrate our wins, it expects them, we are left with a status of expertise and expectations rather than esteem.

If you were doing what you love, you are on the right path. Success and happiness are lining up. You will often be amongst those who arrive first on the field and the last to leave. People love to work with, and for you. You have found your purpose and you leverage conformity to find your Destiny, your place in the Universe.

But to many more amongst us, we are doing the same and yet, we do not feel as happy, as complete. This is because our expertise and wins were not aligned with what we are inside, what we love. All the confidence that we accumulated were still based on what Conformity granted us.

We are champions of resilience, but not whole nor happy. I've been there, I was one lost soul, performing my role in society. Every day feels like a dream where all the ingredients are there but the colours are faded. Then we take measures to address it and the colours are not over saturated.

We can tweak all the settings and yet, it feels so difficult to just reach a state of happiness. This is because you are not whole and are looking in the wrong direction, doing the right things! Ever feel that never-ending kind of dream?

You will break from this course with a few events in your life: finding true love, becoming a parent, losing someone dear. Those are the kind of events that bypass your mind to resonate straight with your heart and make your whole body react.

Remember that the conditioning of Society was ingrained primarily in your mind. Love, birth, death are part of Life, not of Conformity. That is how and why the fog will clear out to leave us to feel deeply, happiness and sadness. And then, our minds will catch up and buffer the emotion.

If we were sad, that will be our salvation. If we were happy, we will somehow convince ourselves that it was a necessary step to preserve happiness… dimming it down. This is just a mindset, a training, a conditioning. Now that you know, it becomes a choice!

"Mindsets, training, and habits are learnt. Now that you know, they become choices!"
Dr. Bak Nguyen

That is quote #2453. In my case, true love lifted me up and allowed me to heal. Then, I took too much time and Conformity sat back in. I will take the birth of my son to kick me out of stasis. My final awakening happened at the death of my grandfather, a man I love as a second dad.

These three events aligned in 15 years. I was in and out of stasis for 15 years, making my way 2 steps forward and one backward. It was finally as my anchors were lifted, a few years later that I just move forward and never looked back. This is how I finally understood the meaning that life only flows forward and that looking back, will just mess will our perception.

Today, I make and celebrate my successes, each day, every day. I elevate myself servicing others, and by extension, Society.

"I do not rebel but I do not wait for permission either."
Dr. Bak Nguyen

That is quote #2454. And that is how I have finally found success after success, building with what is on my path and leveraging the challenge and liability into my next home run.

For those of you wondering how do I do it so fast and repetitively, well, it is because since I stopped tunnel vision, I also stopped seeking for what is not, and I became very aware of what is surrounding me.

"I spent my time making a difference instead of looking for a difference. That's was my key to success and momentum."
Dr. Bak Nguyen

That is quote #2455. So success is really what you make of your day, of your choices. If you ask me, the danger is to accept the only definition of success that Conformity gave us, as success is granted. It is not. Success is earned!

And the more we celebrate success, the more we will be in a position to have better and bigger ones, successes, and celebrations!

What are we celebrating watching the Olympians winning gold medals? His and her determination to inspire us. It is not the fastest time that we are celebrating but the inspiration. Imagine that you can do the same, celebrating your daily victories! You are doing so, not celebrating your solutions but the inspiration to do it again, to do it better.

"Inspiration becomes leverage as it becomes motivation."
Dr. Bak Nguyen

As this quote is #2456. Set yourself for success, not for permission.

This is **Shortcut volume 5, SUCCESS**. Welcome to the Alphas.

PART 2

"104 SUCCESS QUOTES"

by Dr. BAK NGUYEN

2074

FROM SYMPHONY OF SKILLS

"There are no failures until we give up."

Dr. Bak Nguyen

2075

FROM SYMPHONY OF SKILLS

"Nowadays, success doesn't comes from secrecy but rather from successfully sharing knowledge."

Dr. Bak Nguyen

2076

FROM LEADERSHIP, PANDORA'S BOX

"Victory is in the race."

Dr. Bak Nguyen

2077

FROM IDENTITY, ANTHOLOGY OF QUESTS

"Freewill is over rated since one only have the choice to succeed or to fail!"

Dr. Bak Nguyen

2078

FROM IDENTITY, ANTHOLOGY OF QUESTS

"Welcome the end and greet the new beginning."

Dr. Bak Nguyen

2079

FROM IDENTITY, ANTHOLOGY OF QUESTS

"If you want to succeed every single time,
turn your liability into leverage!"

Dr. Bak Nguyen

2080

FROM IDENTITY, ANTHOLOGY OF QUESTS

"Failure is just a statement in time, until we look at the
whole story! The only way it remains a failure it was
because it was the last page of the book."

Dr. Bak Nguyen

2081

FROM IDENTITY, ANTHOLOGY OF QUESTS

"To be is not to think. To be is to do."

Dr. Bak Nguyen

2082

FROM PROFESSION HEALTH

"Don't get blinded by the unexpected nor
be limited by the scope of your own lights."

Dr. Bak Nguyen

2083

"Skills serve hope, every single time."

Dr. Bak Nguyen

2084

"Wisdom is not the cumulation of knowledge.
Wisdom is the knowledge that one knows the way."

Dr. Bak Nguyen

2085

"In finance just like in life, it's not because you didn't
take any decision that the decision was not taking for
you... by a third party. Ignorance is not an option."

Dr. Bak Nguyen

2086

"A disruptor is an entrepreneur who has established a
new benchmark. there will be a before, and after era."

Dr. Bak Nguyen

2087
"Shoot for the moon, that's the best way to minimize the risk-reward ratio."
Dr. Bak Nguyen

2088
"To succeed, one needs to open.
To last, one needs to have fun."
Dr. Bak Nguyen

2089
"No is opportunity."
Dr. Bak Nguyen

2090
"As much as success is a state of mind, business is communication."
Dr. Bak Nguyen

2091
"Raise the average and money will follow."
Dr. Bak Nguyen

2092

" I bet on myself, always."

Dr. Bak Nguyen

2093

" Read people, read the crowd, and then you may have a chance in this game of entrepreneurship."

Dr. Bak Nguyen

2094

" Make it about them, always!"

Dr. Bak Nguyen

2095

"To beat the impossible, find momentum!"

Dr. Bak Nguyen

2096

"Influence will bring success, every single time."

Dr. Bak Nguyen

2097

FROM THE POWER BEHIND THE ALPHA

"To reach a goal, aim straight. "

Dr. Bak Nguyen

2098

FROM MOMENTUM TRANSFER

" No great success can come without the presence of a strong momentum."

Dr. Bak Nguyen

2099

FROM MOMENTUM TRANSFER

" Put peer pressure on your commitment and try to beat the expectations you've set yourself! "

Dr. Bak Nguyen

2100

FROM MOMENTUM TRANSFER

"You are now a force greater than yourself! That's your own personal momentum!"

Dr. Bak Nguyen

2101

FROM HYBRID

"Timing is about execution, the magic
of appealing and succeeding."

Dr. Bak Nguyen

2102

FROM HYBRID

"I rose up finding worth. Better, creating worth!"

Dr. Bak Nguyen

2103

FROM HYBRID

"Momentum is Victory."

Dr. Bak Nguyen

2104

FROM LEVERAGE COMMUNICATION INTO SUCCESS

"Take the easiest and shorter road
to be understood, always."

Dr. Bak Nguyen

2105

FROM LEVERAGE COMMUNICATION INTO SUCCESS

"Communication is about feeling, not words."

Dr. Bak Nguyen

2106

"Not your words, but the tone of your voice
will guide them."

Dr. Bak Nguyen

2107

"In modern words, the body language
is the metadata."

Dr. Bak Nguyen

2108

"Words are for you, your none verbal
and body language are for the others."

Dr. Bak Nguyen

2109

"Intention first and then, communication."

Dr. Bak Nguyen

2110

"Be genuine and act with confidence!
That's the only thing you can do."
Dr. Bak Nguyen

2111

"To leverage communication, be clear,
be genuine, be honest. Then, go all in!"
Dr. Bak Nguyen

2112

FROM FORCES OF NATURE

"Know who you are, know who
you are dealing with, and then, deal!"
Dr. Bak Nguyen

2113

FROM SELFMADE

"Evolution without resistance and success
without a price to pay!"
Dr. Bak Nguyen

2114
FROM SELFMADE
"Everything is much simpler
when you think like a kid."
Dr. Bak Nguyen

2115
FROM SELFMADE
"It takes courage to face failure.
It takes failure to succeed."
Dr. Bak Nguyen

2116
FROM SELFMADE
"Do it now and make the most of what
you have in hand. That's the only good answer."
Dr. Bak Nguyen

2117
FROM SELFMADE
"The day I served, that day I started to succeed."
Dr. Bak Nguyen

2118
FROM SELFMADE
"Money is the result of my becoming.
For as long as I will stay on top,
money will keep pouring in."
Dr. Bak Nguyen

2119

FROM SELFMADE

"To have a million, think like a millionaire…
and that usually not what you think…"
Dr. Bak Nguyen

2120

FROM SELFMADE

"Ask yourself, do you like to win more
than you are scared to fail."
Dr. Bak Nguyen

2121

FROM SELFMADE

"The keys to victory are skillsets and attitude."
Dr. Bak Nguyen

2122

FROM THE POWER OF YES VOLUME TWO

"If emotions lifted my ambitions,
my consistency built my pace to success."
Dr. Bak Nguyen

2123

FROM CHAMPION MINDSET

"To win is a matter of faith in oneself and opinion.
After, it might become knowledge."
Dr. Bak Nguyen

2124
FROM HOW TO WRITE A BOOK IN 30 DAYS
"The fewer filters, the more genuine."

Dr. Bak Nguyen

2125
FROM POWER, EMOTIONAL INTELLIGENCE
"It's hard enough to win and to be ahead.
Don't fight yourself on top of that!"

Dr. Bak Nguyen

2126
FROM POWER, EMOTIONAL INTELLIGENCE
"It's not enough to never give up. One still needs to
be complete to have a chance to win."

Dr. Bak Nguyen

2127
FROM POWER, EMOTIONAL INTELLIGENCE
"The key is to have them feel the right vibe, yours!"

Dr. Bak Nguyen

2128
FROM POWER, EMOTIONAL INTELLIGENCE
"The more one does, the more one will succeed,
every day, day after day."

Dr. Bak Nguyen

2129

FROM BRANDING

"In the lack of a better alternative,
do the best with what you have in hand, today."

Dr. Bak Nguyen

2130

FROM THE POWER OF YES, VOLUME 1

"Whatever past, Gratitude is the only thing I keep,
moving forward."

Dr. Bak Nguyen

2131

FROM HORIZON VOLUME TWO

"The key to a win-win situation is to create
wealth and value."

Dr. Bak Nguyen

2132

FROM HORIZON VOLUME TWO

"Cause and effect, those rules nature, and the world."

Dr. Bak Nguyen

2133

FROM HOW TO NOT FAIL AS A DENTIST

"I take my duty very seriously. Over time, I learnt to laugh about everything else, starting with myself. "

Dr. Bak Nguyen

2134

FROM HOW TO NOT FAIL AS A DENTIST

"The only thing that matter is to do better tomorrow than I did today."

Dr. Bak Nguyen

2135

FROM HOW TO NOT FAIL AS A DENTIST

"Success is a mean, happiness is a result."

Dr. Bak Nguyen

2136

FROM HOW TO NOT FAIL AS A DENTIST

"Expose yourself, take the time, communication will not be a craft or an art, it will be the extension of your soul."

Dr. Bak Nguyen

2137

FROM HOW TO NOT FAIL AS A DENTIST

"Know your function and who you are serving."

Dr. Bak Nguyen

2138
"Wealth, despite all what people might think, is a choice and a value system. It is neither good or bad. But too often, it has served as an excuse to laziness and stupidity."

Dr. Bak Nguyen

2139
"To BE more than to HAVE is fundamental to the difference between asset and liability."

Dr. Bak Nguyen

2140
"Each asset and each liability share mainly the same thread, it is just a matter of how you have put them to use."

Dr. Bak Nguyen

2141
"Whatever you set in your mind to will define your truth."

Dr. Bak Nguyen

2142
"The training was to learn the figures.
The Genius was to know how to leverage
them to achieve victory."

Dr. Bak Nguyen

2143
FROM MASTERMIND
"I am not smarter, just learning on the way.
I do walk and run every day, though."

Dr. Bak Nguyen

2144
FROM MASTERMIND
"People love stories, they can feel them
so they might believe them."

Dr. Bak Nguyen

2145
FROM THE ENERGY FORMULA
"Move forward, a win at a time. Even small, it will
serve as the next ladder. The key is the speed with
which you are moving from ladder to ladder."

Dr. Bak Nguyen

2146

FROM PLAYBOOK INTRODUCTION VOLUME 1

"To be a millionaire, focus on the mindset,
not the money."

Dr. Bak Nguyen

2147

FROM PLAYBOOK INTRODUCTION VOLUME 1

"Success and wealth are consequences of your
entrepreneurial spirit, not its source."

Dr. Bak Nguyen

2148

FROM PLAYBOOK INTRODUCTION VOLUME 1

"Some opportunities if not most, are time-sensitive."

Dr. Bak Nguyen

2149

FROM PLAYBOOK INTRODUCTION VOLUME 2

"Until it is done, it is air. And once it is done,
it is part of the past, and we will have to move on
after the celebrations."

Dr. Bak Nguyen

2150

FROM PLAYBOOK INTRODUCTION VOLUME 2

"Everything is related, and everything makes sense
from one another."

Dr. Bak Nguyen

2151
"Success is no accident. it is a choice."
Dr. Bak Nguyen

2152
"The trap is to confuse reality and the truth."
Dr. Bak Nguyen

2153
"Your are wealthy, you have riches.
Never confuse the two."
Dr. Bak Nguyen

2154
"Every opportunity has its price."
Dr. Bak Nguyen

2155
"Money is not evil, people are.
Money do not smell, ignorance is."
Dr. Bak Nguyen

2156
FROM SUCCESS IS A CHOICE
"It is always the journey that will write your story,
while History is written with results."
Dr. Bak Nguyen

2157
FROM SUCCESS IS A CHOICE
"Find out who you are, master it and then, leverage it.
That's your recipe for success."
Dr. Bak Nguyen

2158
FROM SUCCESS IS A CHOICE
"An opportunity and a risk are basically
the two faces of the same coin."
Dr. Bak Nguyen

2159
FROM THE 90 DAYS CHALLENGE
"Victory is believing in a vision. Touch that feeling
and you will have won already!"
Dr. Bak Nguyen

2160
FROM THE 90 DAYS CHALLENGE
"Fighting' isn't the best way to victory.
It is just the most obvious."
Dr. Bak Nguyen

2161

"Writing about it, is me boldly talking about tomorrow. It makes it real!"

Dr. Bak Nguyen

2162

FROM RISING

"Trust, vision and consistency, those are the recipe to success, the fuel to rise."

Dr. Bak Nguyen

2163

FROM AFTERMATH

"Be proactive will serve you. Being reactive will cost you much more for lesser results."

Dr. Bak Nguyen

2164

FROM AFTERMATH

"Success comes from the mastery of leveraging. Philanthropy is our best leverage to matter."

Dr. Bak Nguyen

2165
FROM RELEVANCY

"This is the renewal, one based on friendship beyond borders, age and prejudices."

Dr. Bak Nguyen

2166
FROM TORNADO

"I served at the best of my ability and then so… and success followed."

Dr. Bak Nguyen

2167
FROM TORNADO

"The easiest wins are those no one knows existed before they were achieved."

Dr. Bak Nguyen

2168
FROM TORNADO

"Fighting is neither winning nor changing. It is just a fight."

Dr. Bak Nguyen

2169

FROM EMPOWERMENT

"Having to choose between being right or winning, I'll choose winning every single time."

Dr. Bak Nguyen

2170

FROM TOUCHSTONE, LEVERAGING TODAY'S PSYCHOLOGICAL SMOG

"Second chances are no myths, they are real. But the window of opportunity is right after the failure. The longer we wait, the narrower the window gets."

Dr. Bak Nguyen

2171

FROM TOUCHSTONE, LEVERAGING TODAY'S PSYCHOLOGICAL SMOG

"Prideless confidence and a taste for adventure, those are your best keystones to leverage yourself and to rise."

Dr. Bak Nguyen

2172

FROM THE RISE OF THE UNICORN VOLUME TWO

"Success is much better appreciated than happiness, at least, from the consumer point of view."

Dr. Bak Nguyen

2173

FROM THE RISE OF THE UNICORN VOLUME TWO

"On the field, to win, one must keep faith
in what isn't yet, but one also needs to be able
to see the truth from the lies."

Dr. Bak Nguyen

2174

FROM THE BOOK OF LEGENDS VOLUME 3

"Engage the interests, and you will
always exceed the expectations."

Dr. Bak Nguyen

2175

FROM THE BOOK OF LEGENDS VOLUME 3

"Leave the power behind and the fatality
of the relationship is gone!"

Dr. Bak Nguyen

2176

FROM MIRRORS

"No success can come from a half recipe."

Dr. Bak Nguyen

2177

FROM MIRRORS

"The more we raise up into the hierarchy of teaching,
lesser is the difference between
a success and a failure."

Dr. Bak Nguyen

This is **Shortcut volume 5, SUCCESS**. Welcome to the Alphas.

Dr. BAK NGUYEN

PART 3
"BUSINESS"
by Dr. BAK NGUYEN

Business is the best thing that ever happened to me. From a second-generation immigrant to a health professional, I was fortunate to pick a profession that, even as hard as it can be, allows the converge of business and medicine.

If I have to be blunt, if it wasn't for the business side, I might not have last that long as a dentist, as a human being. Allow me to explain. Yesterday I came across an old friend from dental school.

We had such a great time back in school. After the initial "How you are doing?" and "You are looking great!", we asked each other about how many days we work in clinics.

We each are very successful dentists, praised and loved by our patients. We each have new skills and have, somehow learnt to be more efficient on the field. But within 20+ years, we are basically holding the same position that our license granted us, 2 decades ago. That hit me at my core.

If we were employed in any other fields, how would we qualify someone holding the same position since his or her graduation? Let stay polite here… And this is what I was, stuck… with labels of success.

Business is a playground. Business is the modern conquest map, one with fewer victims, blood spills, and collaterals. Before, our ancestors raised wars to evolve and conquer. Today, that thirst can be canalized differently in the business world.

No, the business is not just a war field but a playground where the rules are always rewritten, where the weak will be swallowed by the stronger, and in which, pity has no foothold.

That said, it is also the fertile ground for creativity to flourish and be leveraged upon. Business is the only place nowadays where aggressivity (perceived as ambition) can be seen as a good thing. Why?

"Business is amongst the few fields where
one can create value, can create something new
while creating wealth."
Dr. Bak Nguyen

That is quote #2457. From that point on, almost every other field will converge to business. Art became the cinema and the music industry. Science became pharmaceutic and technological powerhouses. Healing and schooling have taken are more subtitle voices but have become huge industries too.

And to each industry, there is a myriad of companies created to support and supply, themselves growing at the pace of ambitions and needs.

"The law of supply and demand has become
the spine of our modern world."
Dr. Bak Nguyen

That is quote #2458. That is how and why **BUSINESS** is blooming and so dynamic. There are so many industries to choose from, so many to discover and all of them need products and services. There is also the never-ending emergence of entirely new industries and companies. Yes, it is a rough world, but one so much bigger than our previous one.

Discovering the Americas, the British started a new trend for their navy enterprises called a **COMPANIES** which allowed them to act as an independent unity (smaller than a nation) while allowing the different contributors (shareholders). Because they are paying their taxes to the government, these companies opened new trade routes and grew to become ambassadors and foreign outposts, are partners to the government. This was a few centuries ago.

Today, companies like Tesla are pushing the boundaries to space and soon, Mars. Companies like Facebook are redefining how we connect, even how we see and label ourselves with its branch Instagram.

With these companies alone, do you have any idea how many companies, self-employed, entrepreneurs, and influencers are gravitating in these eco-systems?

Every time a new industry emerges, it is undiscovered territories and a new **Far West** race begins. In that sense, the advent of the internet was bigger than the discovery of the Americas! Not in death toll but in opportunities. Before the lords of the games were the Kings and Queens. Now, you need only a dream and the determination to serve as many people as possible to rise.

Our richest people on the planet are self-made multi-billionaires seizing the internet race, the space race, and the information revolution.

So if anything, **BUSINESS** is the greatest of opportunities to any of us. It is not safe, but it is surely not scarce. Abundant is the business world. Abundant in all of its meaning and derivatives.

With the abundance of opportunities and the ever-changing world, spinning faster and faster, there are so many more ways to move up the ladders and to gain wealth. I will say that war has become a very costly path. I am not saying that war has vanished but let face it, war is ambition and business. This is what it has always been.

Now, with the democratization of business and entrepreneurship, war is often not the best option to conquer and gain more wealth and power. The other branches of business have proven to be faster and easier rises.

"Modern business and its democratization have reinforced the notion and will for peace."
Dr. Bak Nguyen

That is quote #2459. Ever heard that politics and business do not go well together? Business people are navigating in hard enough trouble waters with their own storms and tsunami, they do not want the instability of war. Even if war can be an opportunity to gain more influence and wealth, it will come with unnecessary risks and delays.

Before power was held at the court of Kings and Queens. Then, it got shared and expand itself to the Parliaments and Congresses of the world. Today, that power is also shared with the presidents of the myriad of industries. Each has its own agenda, ambitions, and risk tolerance. To rage war is simply not as simple as it once was.

"Business is the best democratization method
ever created."
Dr. Bak Nguyen

This quote is #2460. And we are voting with our money, freely and daily. Can you imagine a better democracy? You are not forced or bully into supporting one industry or company, it is your choice. The anti-trust and anti-monopoly laws made sure that we have a choice.

What are you doing with your choice? Because choice is power! As for me, I made these choices and learnt from each of them. First, I consume and buy. Then I look and at what I bought but also why and how I came to buy that specific service or product. I educated myself and I reproduced the pattern, looking in the mirror.

I grew from a customer into a producer instead. My influence and power are directly linked with how many people I am servicing. That's the spine of my growth, of democracy, voting with our dollars!

From a second-generation immigrant, stuck with the deceptions and expectations of Society, of **Conformity**, of my parents, I found my freedom in **BUSINESS**.

"I stand for peace and prosperity."
Dr. Bak Nguyen

This quote is #2461. This is also why, until now, I have turned down, more than once, the opportunity to join power and management. I am serving already, in the biggest democratization of our Society, **BUSINESS**.

You are powerful with each of the choices that you cast. Yield that power and feel the empowerment. You know the secrets and how they got your vote. You too can learn and grow to be on the ticket. And the best of all, **BUSINESS** is not an all or nothing world, not a king of the hill game nor a the winner takes it all.

"Business is vast, abundant and, like the universe,
business is expanding relentlessly
at an accelerating pace."
Dr. Bak Nguyen

Quote #2462. Business is a playground. Business is democracy at its broadest form. Business is freedom. Business is abundance. And above all, Business is a chance for everyone.

This is **Shortcut volume 5, SUCCESS**. Welcome to the Alphas.

PART 4

"136 BUSINESS QUOTES"

by Dr. BAK NGUYEN

0078

FROM SYMPHONY OF SKILLS

"Entrepreneurship, it's a symphony of skills!"

Dr. Bak Nguyen

0079

FROM SYMPHONY OF SKILLS

"Entrepreneurship is a marathon made of everyday sprints, often without any medal."

Dr. Bak Nguyen

0080

FROM REBOOT, TO GROW FROM MIDLIFE CRISIS

"Business has emotions, but only two: Fear and Greed."

Dr. Bak Nguyen

0081

FROM REBOOT, TO GROW FROM MIDLIFE CRISIS

"In business, we only fear to lose what we already have."

Dr. Bak Nguyen

0082

FROM SELFMADE

"Entrepreneurship is not a profession, it is a way of life, a philosophy."

Dr. Bak Nguyen

0083
FROM SELFMADE
"An entrepreneur is often too busy
to notice the milestones."
Dr. Bak Nguyen

0084
FROM SELFMADE
"The worst thing that can trouble
an entrepreneur is doubt."
Dr. Bak Nguyen

0085
FROM SELFMADE
"Entrepreneurship is a philosophy,
so is success and SO is losing."
Dr. Bak Nguyen

0086
FROM THE RISE OF THE UNICORN
"Liability and asset, To be successful in business,
always know which is which."
Dr. Bak Nguyen

0087
FROM THE RISE OF THE UNICORN
"First rule of the new economy,
awareness first and then, traffic."
Dr. Bak Nguyen

0088

FROM THE RISE OF THE UNICORN

"Cash is king. Cash also needs people."

Dr. Bak Nguyen

0089

FROM CHAMPION MINDSET

"Even if an entrepreneur does not have the answer,
trust me, he will be looking for one
and do it without pride."

Dr. Bak Nguyen

0090

FROM CHAMPION MINDSET

"To go further than your horizon
is the first step of an entrepreneur."

Dr. Bak Nguyen

0091

FROM CHAMPION MINDSET

"Entrepreneurship is the path to heal
and to adapt from wounds and mistakes."

Dr. Bak Nguyen

0092

FROM CHAMPION MINDSET

"To make it into the business world, one must adapt."

Dr. Bak Nguyen

0093

"In the business world, the leaders set
the informal rules of the market."

Dr. Bak Nguyen

0094

"I changed the dental industry because
I was grateful and wanted to give back."

Dr. Bak Nguyen

0095

"You multiply your sale looking at the market and you
divide the cost looking into the eyes of your market."

Dr. Bak Nguyen

0096

"In business, time is the main essence."

Dr. Bak Nguyen

0097

"Your word is everything in the business world.
Honour it, but don't be fooled!"

Dr. Bak Nguyen

0098

"A Credit score is not about the debt you owe,
but rather your attitude and habit consuming credit."

Dr. Bak Nguyen

0099

"Learn to leverage your position,
and you will soon be leveraging time itself!"

Dr. Bak Nguyen

0100

"Unfortunately, in business, the straight forward win
is not the one that will always be the norm."

Dr. Bak Nguyen

0101

"What will come out have to be better
and stronger than what came in."

Dr. Bak Nguyen

0102

"Selling is your contribution to the world."

Dr. Bak Nguyen

0103
"To understand the market,
you should be in and out of the market."
Dr. Bak Nguyen

0104
"In business, the real business is the bigger game,
not the trade."
Dr. Bak Nguyen

0105
"The great thing about business is that
you can buy your cards. The richer you are,
the better your cards and your odds."
Dr. Bak Nguyen

0106
"It takes money to make money.
That's not a rule; those are the odds."
Dr. Bak Nguyen

0107
"There is no free money. Only easier ways to some."
Dr. Bak Nguyen

0108

FROM CHAMPION MINDSET

"In business, just like in sport,
never lose sight of the ball, ever!"

Dr. Bak Nguyen

0109

FROM CHAMPION MINDSET

"Entrepreneurship is a game of leadership
and of scoring. If all you do is scoring,
you've missed half of the game!"

Dr. Bak Nguyen

0110

FROM KRYPTO

"In finance, it is not only the quantity of money
available that makes the difference but
the speed of money, the speed of the
exchanges that create wealth."

Dr. Bak Nguyen

0111

FROM POWER, EMOTIONAL INTELLIGENCE

"Ally or foe, you still need to understand
the person in front of you better."

Dr. Bak Nguyen

0112
FROM HOW TO NOT FAIL AS A DENTIST
"Too many confuse the system and the people even if the difference is obvious. Over time the lines blur to the point of merging."

Dr. Bak Nguyen

0113
FROM HOW TO NOT FAIL AS A DENTIST
"Fresh from school, we were all equals in the eyes of a banker and of the financial system."

Dr. Bak Nguyen

0114
FROM HOW TO NOT FAIL AS A DENTIST
"Finance is a language and your credit score, your position in the ladder."

Dr. Bak Nguyen

0115
FROM HOW TO NOT FAIL AS A DENTIST
"Money is neither good nor bad. It's your character and your choices that will make the label."

Dr. Bak Nguyen

0116

"Transparency, consistency and ambition,
those are the threads that bankers love to see."

Dr. Bak Nguyen

0117

"Get your math right! See the big picture
and the bottom line."

Dr. Bak Nguyen

0118

"With your money, only trust the experts once you
know where you are going. You can rely on them for
the how, but never the why the when and the what."

Dr. Bak Nguyen

0119

"Math is math, numbers cannot lie,
is an understatement."

Dr. Bak Nguyen

0120

"Do not confuse an asset and a property."

Dr. Bak Nguyen

0121

"Our emotional intelligence is playing us
when it comes to make the difference between
an asset and a liability."

Dr. Bak Nguyen

0122

"To exchange our time and expertise for money
is no business! It is a job!"

Dr. Bak Nguyen

0123

"Be on the right side of the trade,
and you will turn your life around and give meaning
to all your hard work."

Dr. Bak Nguyen

0124
FROM HOW TO NOT FAIL AS A DENTIST

"Big or small, you are still held to the same standard of excellence."

Dr. Bak Nguyen

0125
FROM HOW TO NOT FAIL AS A DENTIST

"Price and terms, there are two side to each deal."

Dr. Bak Nguyen

0126
FROM HOW TO WRITE A SUCCESSFUL BUSINESS PLAN

"To serve a solution, that's the core of a business."

Dr. Bak Nguyen

0127
FROM HOW TO WRITE A SUCCESSFUL BUSINESS PLAN

"Forget what's sexy, embrace the efficacy instead."

Dr. Bak Nguyen

0128
FROM HOW TO WRITE A SUCCESSFUL BUSINESS PLAN

"Never confuse a need for a market."

Dr. Bak Nguyen

0129

FROM HOW TO WRITE A SUCCESSFUL BUSINESS PLAN

"More important than to know what you are selling is to know who you are talking to."

Dr. Bak Nguyen

0130

FROM HOW TO WRITE A SUCCESSFUL BUSINESS PLAN

"Make a bold promises and keep them. It is the key to any relationship, especially in business."

Dr. Bak Nguyen

0131

FROM HOW TO WRITE A SUCCESSFUL BUSINESS PLAN

"To be prepared, this is the essence of a business plan."

Dr. Bak Nguyen

0132

FROM HOW TO WRITE A SUCCESSFUL BUSINESS PLAN

"Business is not about being right, but much more about being tuned."

Dr. Bak Nguyen

0133
"To succeed, one needs more than a genius idea,
one needs a plan. "

Dr. Bak Nguyen

0134
"In business, the single most important person
is the customer."

Dr. Bak Nguyen

0135
"A website is the best first move
an entrepreneur can take."

Dr. Bak Nguyen

0136
"Forget the free meal, there is no such thing
in business unless you are eating a bait."

Dr. Bak Nguyen

0137

FROM HOW TO WRITE A SUCCESSFUL BUSINESS PLAN

"You are just in the preludes of your relationship with your customers, it is about them, all about them."

Dr. Bak Nguyen

0138

FROM HOW TO WRITE A SUCCESSFUL BUSINESS PLAN

"Think as you do, listen and adapt.
This is the speed of today's business."

Dr. Bak Nguyen

0139

FROM HOW TO WRITE A SUCCESSFUL BUSINESS PLAN

"Don't be cheap nor chicken
when it comes to define your ambitions."

Dr. Bak Nguyen

0140

FROM HOW TO WRITE A SUCCESSFUL BUSINESS PLAN

"Think big and deliver. That's my job."

Dr. Bak Nguyen

0141

"Stick with your logic and your market,
but listen to the market and adapt to its demands
if you want to last."

Dr. Bak Nguyen

0142

"To the world, it might look like ambition.
They were way behind, always. This is the mindset of
a champion and an entrepreneur."

Dr. Bak Nguyen

0143

"Feelings can be transposed in words or numbers.
Usually, the numbers will be of better uses."

Dr. Bak Nguyen

0144

"To have the interest of a FINANCIER,
they must first trust you."

Dr. Bak Nguyen

0145

FROM HOW TO WRITE A SUCCESSFUL BUSINESS PLAN

"Know your audience."

Dr. Bak Nguyen

0146

FROM HOW TO WRITE A SUCCESSFUL BUSINESS PLAN

"Walk them through your plans,
but from their perspective."

Dr. Bak Nguyen

0147

FROM HOW TO WRITE A SUCCESSFUL BUSINESS PLAN

"Today I am secured enough to share, not to sell."

Dr. Bak Nguyen

0148

FROM HOW TO WRITE A SUCCESSFUL BUSINESS PLAN

"Without money, you will have a good idea.
With the right funding, you have a shot
to change the world!"

Dr. Bak Nguyen

0149

FROM HOW TO WRITE A SUCCESSFUL BUSINESS PLAN

"The idea is just the beginning of the journey.
The execution is the plat de resistance."

Dr. Bak Nguyen

0150

"It is not about you anymore, it never was.
It is about the idea and the solution."

Dr. Bak Nguyen

0151

"Be genuine, honest and respectful.
Those are the basis of communication."

Dr. Bak Nguyen

0152

"Trust comes with familiarity."

Dr. Bak Nguyen

0153

"The message must be clear and bold,
and always about them, not you. "

Dr. Bak Nguyen

0154

" Influence and relationship go a long way
in business and in life."

Dr. Bak Nguyen

0155

FROM HOW TO WRITE A SUCCESSFUL BUSINESS PLAN

"To be fair, we, entrepreneurs, have the better trade of that deal. Be aware, be grateful."

Dr. Bak Nguyen

0156

FROM HOW TO WRITE A SUCCESSFUL BUSINESS PLAN

"Action people, action, are ladders to success."

Dr. Bak Nguyen

0157

FROM MINDSET ARMORY

"Greed and fear are powerful emotions hardwired in any of us. Appeal to one or the other, and you will move mountains."

Dr. Bak Nguyen

0158

FROM MINDSET ARMORY

"That little passport to the world wide web is also the most powerful of self-empowerment!"

Dr. Bak Nguyen

0159

FROM MINDSET ARMORY

"The portal is virtual, the work is not,
and the result could be more real!"

Dr. Bak Nguyen

0160

FROM PLAYBOOK INTRODUCTION VOLUME 1

"Cheap is usually never a good option in business."

Dr. Bak Nguyen

0161

FROM PLAYBOOK INTRODUCTION VOLUME 1

"Do not go for the new nor the cheap,
your name is worth more than that."

Dr. Bak Nguyen

0162

FROM PLAYBOOK INTRODUCTION VOLUME 1

"Well, if you are looking to make millions over
millions, aim for the long term."

Dr. Bak Nguyen

0163

FROM PLAYBOOK INTRODUCTION VOLUME 1

"One-nightstands in business will bring you nothing
but long life diseases and regrets."

Dr. Bak Nguyen

0164

FROM PLAYBOOK INTRODUCTION VOLUME 1

"You can't force and forge an entrepreneur out of you. You can only discover what lays within and empower it."

Dr. Bak Nguyen

0165

FROM PLAYBOOK INTRODUCTION VOLUME 1

"Business and entrepreneurial are long term games, to fight for your survival every step of the way is not the way to thrive and to win over the market."

Dr. Bak Nguyen

0166

FROM PLAYBOOK INTRODUCTION VOLUME 1

"Business is a mindset."

Dr. Bak Nguyen

0167

FROM PLAYBOOK INTRODUCTION VOLUME 1

"Business is a team sport."

Dr. Bak Nguyen

0168

FROM PLAYBOOK INTRODUCTION VOLUME 1

"Business is about relationships."

Dr. Bak Nguyen

0169

FROM PLAYBOOK INTRODUCTION VOLUME 1

"In business, time, more than money, is the essence."

Dr. Bak Nguyen

0170

FROM PLAYBOOK INTRODUCTION VOLUME 2

"Business is about mindset, success is about attitude and entrepreneurship, a way of life."

Dr. Bak Nguyen

0171

FROM PLAYBOOK INTRODUCTION VOLUME 2

"Showbiz loves one-man's show, the public loves heroes. Business is no showbiz nor legends, it is a team effort."

Dr. Bak Nguyen

0172

FROM PLAYBOOK INTRODUCTION VOLUME 2

"One feels and live entrepreneurship. You can't learn this one only from books."

Dr. Bak Nguyen

0173

FROM PLAYBOOK INTRODUCTION VOLUME 2

"Focus on making money more than saving money."

Dr. Bak Nguyen

0174
FROM PLAYBOOK INTRODUCTION VOLUME 2
"The bigger your debts, the bigger your credit.
And credits are how the entrepreneurs win their
leverage to buy more and more time."
Dr. Bak Nguyen

0175
FROM PLAYBOOK INTRODUCTION VOLUME 2
"You worked hard to have the chance to work
even harder and smarter! That's the path
of the entrepreneur."
Dr. Bak Nguyen

0176
FROM AMONGST THE ALPHAS, VOLUME 1
"We are the dominant species because we have
learnt to network over time and space."
Dr. Bak Nguyen

0177
FROM AMONGST THE ALPHAS, VOLUME 1
"Mind your goal and its execution,
the rest will follow accordingly."
Dr. Bak Nguyen

0180

"Interests paid will offset your taxable income."

Dr. Bak Nguyen

0181

"Money is money, whatever you earned or borrowed it. What's important is the time component."

Dr. Bak Nguyen

0182

"Taxes are your greatest expanses every year."

Dr. Bak Nguyen

0183

"There is no free money.
But some money is easier than other."

Dr. Bak Nguyen

0184

"In business, your reputation
is your most valuable asset."

Dr. Bak Nguyen

0185

"For as long as the money borrowed creates more value in the future, the deal is great!"

Dr. Bak Nguyen

0186

"Nowadays, whoever can borrow is wealthy, at least for a moment."

Dr. Bak Nguyen

0187

"In business and finance, there is no such thing as the perfect plan. you do, and you readjust."

Dr. Bak Nguyen

0188

"Business and finance are emotions, emotions and math skills combined."

Dr. Bak Nguyen

0189

"That's the trade.
You are trading security for opportunity."

Dr. Bak Nguyen

0200

FROM SUCCESS IS A CHOICE

"There is always two components to each deal, the prices and the terms. Both of them are of equal importance."
Dr. Bak Nguyen

0201

FROM SUCCESS IS A CHOICE

"No offence can ever be successful with a great defence!"
Dr. Bak Nguyen

0202

FROM SUCCESS IS A CHOICE

"Credit is immediate and not taxable."
Dr. Bak Nguyen

0203

FROM SUCCESS IS A CHOICE

"The mistake is not to be too late but to wait for a better alternative that might never show up."
Dr. Bak Nguyen

0204

FROM RISING

"The destiny of an entrepreneur is to have the means to build his never-ending dream."
Dr. Bak Nguyen

0205

FROM AFTERMATH

"The only way to avoid a global recession
is to expand our openness and connectivity,
not retracting them!"

Dr. Bak Nguyen

0206

FROM AFTERMATH

"Philanthropy was my way out from my own success,
my own prison."

Dr. Bak Nguyen

0207

FROM AFTERMATH

"God made us all unique and different.
We each have a different key to ignite.
Ours is Greed, in a better word, ambition."

Dr. Bak Nguyen

0208

FROM THE POWER OF DR

"There is no free money.
All money has its price."

Dr. Bak Nguyen

0209

"Writing about women entrepreneurs,
I must admit that women are made
much stronger than men."

Dr. Bak Nguyen

0210

FROM BOOTCAMP

"Asset and liability are two faces of the same coin."

Dr. Bak Nguyen

0211

FROM BOOTCAMP

"More than just to be or not to be,
to leave what we know and what we currently are
behind for a hope, not even a promise,
that's entrepreneurship."

Dr. Bak Nguyen

0212

FROM POWERPLAY

"Entrepreneurs are builders.
Empower the entrepreneurs and you have
a driving force leading with hope
and concrete solutions."

Dr. Bak Nguyen

0213

FROM POWERPLAY

"If you buy cheap expertise
it is not a glass half full that you are buying,
it is often the wrong glass to drink from."

Dr. Bak Nguyen

This is **Shortcut volume 5, SUCCESS**. Welcome to the Alphas.

Dr. BAK NGUYEN

PART 5
"THE POWER OF QUOTES"
by Dr. BAK NGUYEN

If we have spent 5 journeys (books) healing, growing, rising, **SUCCESS** was surely a goal to every and any one of us. If success is a universal goal **BUSINESS** is a prime playground to express your power and freedom to Abundance and Happiness.

That was my path, from the son of an immigrant to a doctor in dental medicine to a CEO and from there, from a CEO to a world record author and motivational speak, I found my liberty looking for power walking the path of entrepreneurship.

Each of the words I am sharing with you, I walked. Everyone is looking for secrets and recipes to success, well within these quotes, you have my path, mindsets, regrets, and secrets.

As I said before, there is no way to cheat a quote. You know or you don't. In success, there is no middle either, you win or you don't. That said, win and learn. It is simple and yet, so hard to keep that mindset.

You can also lose and learn. This is pretty hard on the morale but somehow, the lessons sink in much faster! So win or learn, it's a win-win situation. With this, let jump into

8 of these 77 famous Dr. Bak's quotes, 8 to respect the number of the dragon.

FAMOUS QUOTE 1

0010
FROM INDUSTRIES' DISRUPTORS
"Make leverage of each of your liabilities,
and you will always be moving forward."
Dr. Bak Nguyen

Win or learn. That's a perfect example of this mindset. Remember that your most precious resource is time. You are there already, don't look too far, even if the grass seems greener, that might be true, you be spending time walking there just to verify! That's my certainty, based on time, not maybe.

So to make leverage out of this mindset, I look around and act with what is within reach, because I have to act now. I'll be learning and growing doing, so now is always the right timing, and tomorrow, well, that will be tomorrow's now.

I do my best with what I have in hand and the given time. And when the time is running out, it is time to acknowledge the win or the loss, to celebrate, to learn, and to move on. That's growing.

That said, how do you choose what to do in order to grow? Well, I act on what I know best, myself and my surrounding. All around, each flaw, each injustice, each imperfection is an opportunity to jump and to be creative and passionate.

Leveraging others' pains into opportunity, well, I was trained to do just that as a doctor. We call that healing. Each time, their pain, I felt and I eased. They love me for it as they empowered my power and influence voting, not only with their dollars but also with their trust and friendship. I became influential, serving. I was leveraging their liabilities, their pain.

There is nothing wrong with that wording, it was my responsibility, my nobility as a doctor. And then, I realized that we are complaining a lot, but a lot, about the inefficiencies, the injustices, the waiting… all of those are pains, not personal but societal pains.

I started to address those too, approaching them as a doctor, identifying a factor that I can surgically influence to change the outcome. From a dentist, I rose to a CEO and an industry's disruptor.

I did not wait to be perfect to take care of others nor did I wait for Society to ask for my help. I was present and people came asking for my assistance. First with their pains, then, with their desires and dreams. I made the most of each moment, leveraging their problems to help them grow. In the process, I grew even more.

As I was helping others, I applied the same process to solve my own pains and dreams. It was then that I noticed that taking care of other's pain is much easier than to deal with your own. Dealing with other's problems, there is no denial or emotions. These 2 will be eating much of the brainpower we have available.

Looking for the perfect solution is also a huge eater of our resources. The clock is ticking, we need a solution, an improvement over the current situation. Well, if looking for the best solution sounds like the perfect course of action, you still need to consider the time needed in investment.

Most of the time, an ok and imperfect solution is much better than the perfect solution… since you will have to come back anyway for maintenance, upgrades, and patches anyway. And if you don't, well, sooner or later, what you thought permanent and eternal will break down and be replaced.

And that's the liability I am looking for: what can I replace, improve or upgrade before it breaks. If I am doing it before it breaks, I still call the shots, I am in control.

And you know what? If easing other's people pain made me into a good and noble doctor, well, solving my own pains, I was on my own. The road was long and dreadful. Sharing what I learnt in the process and easing you through your own journey elevated me to international status, world record writer, and into an Alpha. I started addressing liabilities, yours and then, mine.

FAMOUS QUOTE 2

0013
FROM INDUSTRIES' DISRUPTORS
"Be mindful of the consequences."
Dr. Bak Nguyen

Actually, this is from my 20 years + serving as a doctor. As a doctor, the rule is simple, do no harm. And yet, we are surgeons, we are cutting and replacing. The trade is always to gain more than we lose. There is no way no can do that if one tunnels vision too narrowly. It is about the big picture, always the big picture.

Well, what sounded logical and set by default in medicine, in life and in business, this was not something people are used to. I am not saying that everyone has no conscience but we often think that it is not our problem to care, even if what we do is worsening the situation.

I learnt that lesson in politics as I was in training. Whatever problem I am addressing in society, I am also tackling a delicate balance. First, the pain of the problem must be greater than the pain of change (the pain of implementing the solution) to have a chance of success.

But no matter who one will tackle this one, there is always resistance, even if you are doing it for the common good. I told you that democracy is great and a thing of many. Well, in the many, each has their own agenda, goals, and views.

So, no matter what you are doing, there is no solution that will keep everyone happy. It is now a matter of number, you help the majority. This does not mean that the minority can simply be forgotten. And here is the true lesson in this quote.

To make a difference, we need actions.
Action has consequences.
The more the negative consequences,
The more collaterals
The greater the resistance.
Even worse, the rise of your nemesis.

Some nemesis will make their life work to simply erase what you have done. I am too lazy to fall into that never-ending game. I prefer to be as **compassionate** as possible and to move as **quickly** as possible. I understand my ripple effects and always weigh the wins with the collaterals.

"At the end of the day, both, wins and collaterals are making their way into your ledger."
Dr. Bak Nguyen

That's quote #2463. Yes, that's a new one.

0017
FROM CHANGING THE WORLD FROM A DENTAL CHAIR
"Make it happen!"
Dr. Bak Nguyen

Can it be any clearer than this? If you want something, make it happen. Don't count on anybody else but yourself. If, like me, what you are doing is to ease pain and empowering dreams, do it without looking back. Make sure to understand the ripple effect of your actions and be ready to face their consequences (if you did not mind carefully the pros and the cons).

That said, that materialize when I stopped asking for permission. As a doctor, my patients are demanding for my help. The beginning of my journey with them is a permission.

Addressing Society, we are all concerned and management is often too proud to ask for help anyway. In societal issues, I feel that it is my responsibility to take care of my home, of my people. I do not wait for permission.

I don't tackle everything all at once either. I wait for what I can change and impact. Then, I act as swiftly as possible and I move on. The longer I will be caught in, the more the resistance and liability will resonate. This is a law of physic. All of that starts with you, as you make it happen, as you are taking action.

"No action, no change. The consequences
will still have to be dealt with."
Dr. Bak Nguyen

That's quote #2464. Know your strength and care. Care for yourself, care for others and bet on yourself. Make it happen and then, react to your own consequences. The swifter the intervention, the fewer the complications (a law of surgery), the fewer the resistance (a law of physics).

Know yourself, know the laws of the universe and find your worth, today!

0035
FROM THE RISE OF THE UNICORN
"A Momentum is when it is easier
to keep moving than to stop."
Dr. Bak Nguyen

This is probably one of my most powerful quotes, once you have started. You know that saying of: "You don't have to be great to start but you need to start to be great." from the Olympics 2020 commercials, well, that is right on point.

Actions change the hormones produced in your body. Your body is reacting to these hormones and will start to feel different, will have hunger that was dormant until that point. In other words, start and you will discover new desires and needs. Is that bad? In at all! This is what will push you forward, to walk and seek what you did not know even existed before.

So when I am saying that a momentum is reached as it becomes easier to keep moving than to stop, I am not exaggerating. It is not even a superpower reserved for a few privileged. It is the normal response of our body to actions.

And we all know that actions have consequences. Stand up and face the consequences of your actions, good and bad. React to them and what will happen next? You are, once again in action, to either double down on a victory or to fix a mistake. Either way, you are back in action almost immediately. And more hormones will be produced.

Soon enough, your body will be craving for these hormones of actions, called endorphins, and just like the athletes, you will push yourself harder and harder to feel that supreme sensation of wellbeing once more. You are growing.

Is that an addiction? Yes, you are now addicted to action, to success, to matter. Wasn't that the top of the pyramid of Maslow? Wasn't that what you were looking for?

The secret here is to start, no matter where you currently stand. The power is to react, no matter the consequences. And the remedy is that you have killed procrastination once and for all with your new addiction. You are rising!

0036
FROM CHAMPION MINDSET
"I was open, and I bet on myself."
Dr. Bak Nguyen

This is my personal story but one everyone can learn and leverage from. As I was reaching the glass ceiling of the pyramid of Maslow, stuck at belonging, I knew that I was destined for more. My whole body was demanding for more, for better.

I stood up and reshaped my company of 15 years, Mdex, to now serve my industry, the dental industry. Instead of beating the average, I pivoted and was now dedicated to help my peers and formal competition. For that, I needed a reset from my old mindsets and values. I decided to reboot myself, saying yes to virtually everything, for 18 months.

During that time, I met with a crazy producer. The man is brilliant, he has ideas that were out of this world. Well, to introduce me as a speaker to the world, he booked me a spot to talk after the former first lady of the USA. I was not just intimidated, I was shitting my pants! But I was also too proud to admit it.

I said yes and I will honour my word. I went home and got prepared, writing Ted Talks. By the way, English is not my first language. I am a French-speaking person and I think in French first, then, I have to translate my words and thoughts. Needless to tell you how uncomfortable I was.

Michelle Obama put fear in my heart and I ran to face the consequences of my action: saying YES. Well, long story short, Michelle Obama never made the speaking event for administrative reasons… but I was ready. I wrote a first Ted Talk, then, another, and another.

Ted Talks became chapters and chapters became books. Today, I am a world record writer, with close to 100 books under my belt within the last 4 years. If it wasn't for that producer, I may not have even started my first book yet. I say YES and then, I bet on myself!

"Action and consequence. That's all you need to start."
Dr. Bak Nguyen

That's quote #2465.

FAMOUS QUOTE 6

0040
FROM POWER, EMOTIONAL INTELLIGENCE
"Align your emotions and your ambitions
to be whole, to be unstoppable."
Dr. Bak Nguyen

Before you can reach momentum, you need to find the power to propel yourself. Well, that power is found in your belly. Not your stomach, your belly!

I am talking about your sensations, your needs, your desires, and your emotions. If we are very aware of the difference between an emotion and a thought, we are often confusing emotions and sensations. Well, for the sake of this conversation, let put them all in the same melting pot, sensations, and emotions.

You are what you feel. Or you feel what you are. That said, that is the only truth you will ever find. Our training and education have conditioned us to do what is in our head, not what is in our heart, even less, what is felt ever deeper, in our guts. That's how Conformity emancipated us all, one at a time.

But it could not carve our instincts and feeling out, the best it could do was to mute it with what it could control, our minds. Well, we still have access to all of the truth and power within us. Think of your emotions and sensation as a wild animal, your power animal. That's your ride.

First, you need to be aware of its presence and to acknowledge it. Then, it is about getting to know one another and to learn to be in synergy. If your emotions were a wild stallion, caged for years, will you let it out in your living room for its first release? If you do, it will rip off your house completely just to stretch its legs!

You go in the wild where there is no one around, where the air is fresh, and where the sky touches the earth. Then, you let it out. The Stallion will burst out of its cage. It will run and run and run. Eventually, it will run tire and will come back to you. Why? Because it is part of a you. Now, you can talk and get acquainted.

Spend enough time to know your emotions (yourself) and you are now much more powerful. First, because you are saving on all the energy you previously spent on keeping the stallion in cage. Secondly, you now have a ride to surf your journey. And guess what? You have more than one emotion to know and to ride!

Can you feel the power now? Align your emotions (your feelings) and your ambitions (your goals) and you will be riding for glory before you know!

FAMOUS QUOTE 7

0049
FROM HOW TO NOT FAIL AS A DENTIST
"I am not giving up, I am simply wising up!"
Dr. Bak Nguyen

In most of my books, you can read me saying to embrace action, to keep pushing, to make it happen. That's how one starts. Can we keep winning with that mindset? Not always.

Younger, if someone put a wall in front of me and it was either it or me. I grew up strong and very good at knocking walls down. Then, I also notice that I wasn't moving pretty fast. Each victory brought me more trouble than glory. Resistance was mainly my prize…

"Knocking down walls after walls, resistance was my prize. More price than prize."
Dr. Bak Nguyen

That's quote #2466. Then, I learnt to be lazy, to surf the flow instead of fighting it. I wised up and put my head down. It took me a few years but I finally learnt to **surf** the change instead of knocking down the walls. I found new superpowers, speed and momentum.

Today, my momentum can knock down most of the walls that I know, almost effortlessly. But now, I know better. I try to not do that. That will be a last resort. I know how and because I know, I will try not to do that.

Instead, I will try to find more subtle ways to help and inspire change, empowering people and hope. Why? Because it will create less resistance and, if a change is made, it might have a chance to last.

Since I am now empowering more than knocking down walls, I am also waiting for people to act. And since I do not believe in forcing people, I can't either force or push an idea. I will simply inspire and empower.

I will hold the flag but it will be for the people, each one of the people to decide to join or not. If the momentum is there, I will be pushing. If not, I will move on until the time is right. I am not giving up, just listening to the will of the people.

FAMOUS QUOTE 8

0038
FROM HOW TO WRITE A BOOK IN 30 DAYS
"A quote is a truth from another life, from a past legacy."
Dr. Bak Nguyen

That is what I thought, reading quotes of great minds that came before me. And then, I realized that quotes are not just the condensed summary of a thought but a great way to validate one's thought.

You see, I write quotes as I breathe. I do so because it allows me to hear my thoughts resonating in time and to have a chance to react to them. An idea, to be great, to last, needs to have a practical application, usefulness.

Well, comprising your thoughts within a quote will do just that, to see if that mindset can become a recipe to ease others' journey.

While hearing the echo of that same quote, it also gives me the chance to feel the potential ripple effects and to foresee the consequences. That's how I validate a mindset.

So yes, a quote is a truth from another life but it is also the simulation of a possible future, your future!

This is **Shortcut volume 5, SUCCESS**. Welcome to the Alphas.

PART 6

"FAMOUS QUOTES"

by Dr. BAK NGUYEN

0001

FROM SYMPHONY OF SKILLS

"The pain of the problem has to be greater than the pain of change."

Dr. Bak Nguyen

0002

FROM SYMPHONY OF SKILLS

"Sharing is the way to grow."

Dr. Bak Nguyen

0003

FROM LEADERSHIP, PANDORA'S BOX

"One's legend can only begin the day one's Quest of Identity is over."

Dr. Bak Nguyen

0004

FROM IDENTITY, ANTHOLOGY OF QUESTS

"Gratitude is the only past with a future."

Dr. Bak Nguyen

0005

FROM PROFESSION HEALTH

"Mine was, forgive yourself."

Dr. Bak Nguyen

0006
"To walk on thin ice is a dangerous game.
To run is safer. To surf is the easiest."
Dr. Bak Nguyen

0007
"If I have changed the world from a dental chair,
you are all in a better position than I am
to change the world."
Dr. Bak Nguyen

0008
"The day you are fighting to raise the average instead
of beating it, that day, you've joined the leadership."
Dr. Bak Nguyen

0009
"At the end of the day, business is communication."
Dr. Bak Nguyen

0010

"Make leverage of each of your liabilities,
and you will always be moving forward."

Dr. Bak Nguyen

0011

"I believe in myself and I do it for God,
not the other way around."

Dr. Bak Nguyen

0012

"Always choose the path of least resistance."

Dr. Bak Nguyen

0013

"Be mindful of the consequences."

Dr. Bak Nguyen

0014

"Hammering air three times over and
it will become steel."

Dr. Bak Nguyen

0015
FROM CHANGING THE WORLD FROM A DENTAL CHAIR
"Mdex, for joy for life."
Dr. Bak Nguyen

0016
FROM CHANGING THE WORLD FROM A DENTAL CHAIR
"Confidence is sexy."
Dr. Bak Nguyen

0017
FROM CHANGING THE WORLD FROM A DENTAL CHAIR
"Make it happen!"
Dr. Bak Nguyen

0018
FROM THE POWER BEHIND THE ALPHA
"Humility is to know what you are and
to recognize what you are not."
Dr. Bak Nguyen

0019
FROM MOMENTUM TRANSFER
"On thin ice, speed up, that's how you will
eventually learn to fly! "
Dr. Bak Nguyen

0020

FROM MOMENTUM TRANSFER

"Control with wisdom is called influence."

Dr. Bak Nguyen

0021

FROM MOMENTUM TRANSFER

"To stabilize a momentum, speed up!"

Dr. Bak Nguyen

0022

FROM HYBRID

"Chords and patterns are the themes of the Universe."

Dr. Bak Nguyen

0023

FROM HYBRID

"A weakness is a strength out of reach."

Dr. Bak Nguyen

0024

FROM HYBRID

"Look for your next immediate win."

Dr. Bak Nguyen

0025

FROM REBOOT, TO GROW FROM MIDLIFE CRISIS

"Don't stop the flow of a river unless you are ready to clean up the flood."

Dr. Bak Nguyen

0026

FROM LEVERAGE COMMUNICATION INTO SUCCESS

"Find your worth in the service of others."

Dr. Bak Nguyen

0027

FROM LEVERAGE COMMUNICATION INTO SUCCESS

"Humility is not the denial of oneself but the acceptance of one true nature."

Dr. Bak Nguyen

0028

FROM THE BOOK OF LEGENDS, VOLUME 1

"We are all born little, as a chicken heart. If we keep an open mind, we will grow into a lion heart. Some will choose to be close-minded and will remain small."

Dr. Bak Nguyen

0029

FROM THE BOOK OF LEGENDS, VOLUME 1

"To have an open mind is step one.
To keep growing, one needs an open heart."
Dr. Bak Nguyen

0030

FROM THE BOOK OF LEGENDS, VOLUME 1

"Humility is the ability to recognize and to respect
what we are, and stop pretending to be
what we are not."
Dr. Bak Nguyen

0031

FROM SELFMADE

"Good things start to happen when you say yes!"
Dr. Bak Nguyen

0032

FROM SELFMADE

"Knowledge is the ground of the past.
Hope and Dreams are the air of the future."
Dr. Bak Nguyen

0033

FROM SELFMADE

"My deepest fear is to show up before God
and not have enough to show for."
Dr. Bak Nguyen

0034

FROM THE RISE OF THE UNICORN

"To make the world a better place."

Dr. Bak Nguyen

0035

FROM THE RISE OF THE UNICORN

"A Momentum is when it is easier
to keep moving than to stop."

Dr. Bak Nguyen

0036

FROM CHAMPION MINDSET

"I was open, and I bet on myself."

Dr. Bak Nguyen

0037

FROM HOW TO WRITE A BOOK IN 30 DAYS

"To keep Momentum, aim for the next win,
as little as it might be."

Dr. Bak Nguyen

0038

FROM HOW TO WRITE A BOOK IN 30 DAYS

"A quote is a truth from another life,
from a past legacy."

Dr. Bak Nguyen

0039
FROM HOW TO WRITE A BOOK IN 30 DAYS
"The fewer the words, the better."

Dr. Bak Nguyen

0040
FROM POWER, EMOTIONAL INTELLIGENCE
"Align your emotions and your ambitions
to be whole, to be unstoppable."

Dr. Bak Nguyen

0041
FROM POWER, EMOTIONAL INTELLIGENCE
"I believe in myself, and I do it for God,
not the other way around."

Dr. Bak Nguyen

0042
FROM BRANDING
"I kept the "Dr." on to remind me to always
put your interests before mine."

Dr. Bak Nguyen

0043
FROM BRANDING
"Arrogance is not the bragging of our knowledge,
but rather the denial of our ignorance."

Dr. Bak Nguyen

0044

FROM HORIZON VOLUME ONE

"I treat people, not teeth."

Dr. Bak Nguyen

0045

FROM THE POWER OF YES, VOLUME 1

"Writing books allowed me to evolve
at the speed of my thoughts."

Dr. Bak Nguyen

0046

FROM THE POWER OF YES, VOLUME 1

"Speed is my power. Momentum, my expression."

Dr. Bak Nguyen

0047

FROM THE POWER OF YES VOLUME 3

"We do not need to choose, only to prioritize."

Dr. Bak Nguyen

0048

FROM HOW TO NOT FAIL AS A DENTIST

"Changing the world from a dental chair."

Dr. Bak Nguyen

0049

FROM HOW TO NOT FAIL AS A DENTIST

"I am not giving up, I am simply wising up!"

Dr. Bak Nguyen

0050

FROM HOW TO NOT FAIL AS A DENTIST

"With your money, do not trust anyone but yourself."

Dr. Bak Nguyen

0051

FROM HUMILITY FOR SUCCESS

"Reading will be cool again!"

Dr. Bak Nguyen

0052

FROM HUMILITY FOR SUCCESS

"Until it is done, it is air, good air but only air."

Dr. Bak Nguyen

0053

FROM MASTERMIND

"You can cheat, legally, by learning about shortcuts and leveraging."

Dr. Bak Nguyen

0054

FROM PLAYBOOK INTRODUCTION VOLUME 1

"Nothing will last forever, and nothing is free."

Dr. Bak Nguyen

0055

FROM PLAYBOOK INTRODUCTION VOLUME 2

"Be careful since doubts is a pet
that you are feeding."

Dr. Bak Nguyen

0056

FROM PLAYBOOK INTRODUCTION VOLUME 2

"Reach for your next win as soon as possible,
and build on it!"

Dr. Bak Nguyen

0057

FROM AMONGST THE ALPHAS, VOLUME 2

"Be bold, confident, and humble."

Dr. Bak Nguyen

0058

FROM AMONGST THE ALPHAS, VOLUME 2

"Growth happens at the giving end,
not the receiving one."

Dr. Bak Nguyen

0059
FROM SUCCESS IS A CHOICE
"Be bold, be flexible, act fast and stay humble."
Dr. Bak Nguyen

0060
FROM SUCCESS IS A CHOICE
"To succeed, be flexible."
Dr. Bak Nguyen

0061
FROM 90 DAYS CHALLENGE
"In times of crisis, one has to reinvent oneself."
Dr. Bak Nguyen

0062
FROM RISING
"To matter, serve."
Dr. Bak Nguyen

0063
FROM RISING
"There is no free money."
Dr. Bak Nguyen

0064
FROM AFTERMATH
"For the first time of our lifetime,
all the interests of the world are aligned."
Dr. Bak Nguyen

0065

FROM AFTERMATH

"In times of crisis, it is the perfect opportunity
to reinvent who we are. "

Dr. Bak Nguyen

0066

FROM AFTERMATH

"Yes, we can have it all!"

Dr. Bak Nguyen

0067

FROM TORNADO

"History will say that to celebrate one world record,
we scored two more!"

Dr. Bak Nguyen

0068

FROM TORNADO

"The only way to keep overdelivering
is playing, all-in!"

Dr. Bak Nguyen

0069

FROM TORNADO

"Dream and the means will come."

Dr. Bak Nguyen

0070

FROM ALPHA LADDERS VOLUME ONE

"All good things start with a YES."

Dr. Bak Nguyen

0071

FROM ALPHA LADDERS VOLUME 2

"Growth occurs at the giving end, always."

Dr. Bak Nguyen

0072

FROM THE CONFESSION OF AN OVERACHIEVER

"Being lazy doesn't mean that you don't have to do shit, it means that you don't have to go through shit to get things done."

Dr. Bak Nguyen

0073

FROM TO OVERACHIEVE EVERYTHING BEING LAZY

"Arrogance is not the recognition of who we are but the denial of what we are not."

Dr. Bak Nguyen

0074
FROM TO OVERACHIEVE EVERYTHING BEING LAZY
"You call me doctor to remind me to always put your needs before mine."
Dr. Bak Nguyen

0075
FROM TO OVERACHIEVE EVERYTHING BEING LAZY
"Nowadays, influence is power without liability."
Dr. Bak Nguyen

0076
FROM TO OVERACHIEVE EVERYTHING BEING LAZY
"I told you that everything in life is a trade. Be careful of what you are trading."
Dr. Bak Nguyen

0077
FROM SHORTCUT VOLUME 1 - HEALING
"Fear is a disease and it must be treated like one."
Dr. Bak Nguyen

This is **Shortcut volume 2, GROWTH**. Welcome to the Alphas.

Dr. BAK NGUYEN

CONCLUSION
by Dr. BAK NGUYEN

This is the third volume about **RISING** in the **SHORTCUT series**, after **LEADERSHIP** and **CONFIDENCE**. **SUCCESS** is what resonates in the mind of each of us, looking forward. Is it? The answer is a little more complicated than that.

At first glance, we might all be looking to succeed, that's how we rise and move up the ladders of life (well described in the pyramid of Maslow). But then have you noticed that you often reproduce the souvenirs of your childhood? Why is that?

Because we were happy once. The irony of our faith is to walk all of the journey, healing, growing, rising to end up looking for what we had at birth, happiness. I am not saying that you are not happy now. But yet, you are walking the journey that will bring you home.

Your parents gave you love and protection. You love them too. But only when you are becoming a parent yourself, will you be returning the favour to your children. Them, in turn, will do the same, giving their love forward. The only thing going back is **Gratitude**, and that is not one to miss.

"The only past with a future is Gratitude."
Dr. Bak Nguyen

And this is the essence of **SUCCESS,** if you ask me. Success is to achieve and to move on. You are looking back only to say thank you and then, to turn your head as quickly as possible looking ahead. That's your first rule of success, not to work hard, not to learn, not to never give up. Your first rule of success is to move forward and to show and feel gratitude.

Now, you are moving forward with a *legacy*, the legacy of how to give and how to receive. From there, welcome Life and its challenges (liabilities), those, you will turn into an asset, leveraging yourself to outgrow each of them.

As you are looking for liabilities, here's a great secret: it is easier for you to leverage and heal the liabilities of others than your own. The *"mind your own business"* mindset is a corruption of your code.

"To care for others is always easier than
to care for yourself."
Dr. Bak Nguyen

That's quote #2467. It is easier and faster because you do not have to deal with your own denials nor emotions. Your emotions will be only attached with the outcome and journey but the growth is happening just as much.

That's what I taught you in **SHORTCUT volume 3, LEADERSHIP**, that's where I told you to start. Now you understand the mechanism behind the logic.

Keep giving and you will be growing.
Keep an open mind
And you will be growing at each step.
Keep an open heart
And you will expand your storage space
To grow even more!

"Success is not a destiny but a journey."
Dr. Bak Nguyen

If your final goal is success, what will you do once you arrived? You will be waiting for your expiration date to come and get you? Even worse, while waiting, you will simply decay and be the victim of your own ambitions.

Success is a journey, a never-ending journey for most. That said, success can also serve as ladders, stepping stones to move faster and higher. That's why I told you to move forward to your next win, as soon as possible.

Those are not only stepping stones but your best leverage to upgrade. And where the **upgrades** are coming from? Well, your body, from the hormones that it will produce as you are in action.

I don't know about you but to me, that's how and when I feel at my best, that I am happy, with **endorphins**. And after a surge in endorphins, your body goes back in craving mode until your next win. What you are keeping from the experience is the confidence that you can do it and the skills gained in the process. Well, that was the journey, growing from one win to the next.

From all the fields of Life, Business was the best field that I found to exert success. Business because of the freedom it provides, the abundance possible, and the myriad of opportunities. I am not saying that business is the only ground to exert success but this is what I know. That field has been very good to me.

And when will I stop? When will you stop? I am tempted to say never but since I learnt to nuance my positions, I will say not yet! Moving from one win to the next, now I have the skills to enjoy the way and to have fun jumping and discovering.

I jump and surf because I started. I started because I was looking to heal. Then I grew, giving (that was the best way to beat resistance). The more I gave, the bigger and faster I grew. My growth became my rise.

I kept rising thanks to my Confidence and from there, I attracted success to me. Until that point in my life, I was chasing **SUCCESS**. I had a few wins, sure, but that was not easy and I found no leverage to stack them up to move faster or higher.

"Attracting success is your best course of action.
Don't go out chasing it."
Dr. Bak Nguyen

I welcome, I provoke but I stopped chasing a long time ago. I am not chasing success, I am jumping from a challenge to the next. That's the idea.

The next phase of **RISING** is to deal with the consequences of **SUCCESS**, **POWER**. To each action, its consequence. Now that you have reached success, you are holding and/or stepping on powers beyond your understanding.

I told you that **RISING** was the best part! Well, this is a story for another journey. See you soon, in **volume 6, POWER**!

This is **Shortcut volume 5, SUCCESS**. Welcome to the Alphas.

Dr. BAK NGUYEN

ANNEX
GLOSSARY OF Dr. BAK's LIBRARY

1

1SELF -080

REINVENT YOURSELF FROM ANY CRISIS
BY Dr. BAK NGUYEN

In 1SELF is about to reinvent yourself to rise from any crisis. Written in the midst of the COVID war, now more than ever, we need hope and the know-how to bridge the future. More than just the journey of Dr. Bak, this time, Dr. Bak is sharing his journey with mentors and people who built part of the world as we know it. Interviewed in this book, CHRISTIAN TRUDEAU, former CEO and FOUNDER of BCE EMERGIS (BELL CANADA), he also digitalized the Montreal Stock Exchange.RON KLEIN, American Innovator, inventor of the magnetic stripe of the credit card, of MLS (Multi-listing services) and the man who digitalized WALL STREET bonds markets.ANDRE CHATELAIN, former first vice-president of the MOVEMENT DES JARDINS. Dr. JEAN DE SERRES, former CEO of HEMA QUEBEC. These men created billions in values and have changed our lives, even without us knowing. They all come together to share their experiences and knowledge to empower each and everyone to emerge stronger from this crisis, from any crisis.

A

AFTERMATH -063
BUSINESS AFTER THE GREAT PAUSE
BY Dr. BAK NGUYEN & Dr. ERIC LACOSTE

In AFTERMATH, Dr. Bak joins forces with Community leader and philanthrope Dr. Eric Lacoste. Two powerful minds and forces of nature in the reaction to the worst economic meltdown in modern times. We are all victims of the CORONA virus. Both just like humans have learned to adapt to survive, so is our economy. Most business structures and management philosophies are inherited from the age of industrialization and beyond. COVID-19 has shut down the world economy with months. At the time of the AFTERMATH, the truth is many corporations and organizations will either have to upgrade to the INFORMATION AGE or disappear. More than the INFORMATION upgrade, the era of SOCIAL MEDIA and the MILLENNIALS are driving a revolution in the core philosophy of all organizations. Profit is not king anymore, support is. In this time and age where a teenager with a social account can compete with the million dollars PR firm, social implication is now the new cornerstone. Those who will adapt will prevail and prosper, while the resistance and old guards will soon be forgotten as fossils of a past era.

ALPHA LADDERS -075
CAPTAIN OF YOUR DESTINY
BY Dr. BAK NGUYEN & JONAS DIOP

In ALPHA LADDERS, Dr. Bak is sharing his private conversation and board meetings with 2 of his trusted lieutenants, strategist Jonas Diop and international Counsellor, Brenda Garcia. As both the Dr. Bak and ALPHA brands are gaining in popularity and traction, it was time to get the movement to the next level. Now, it's about building a community and to help everyone willing to become ALPHAS to find their powers. Dr. Bak is a natural recruiter of ALPHAS and peers. He also spent the last 20 years plus, training and mentoring proteges. Now comes the time to empower more and more proteges to become ALPHAS. ALPHAS LADDERS is the journey of how Dr. Bak went from a product of Conformity to rise into a force of Nature, know as a kind tornado. In ALPHA LADDERS Jonas pushed Dr. Bak to retrace each of the steps of his awakening, steps that we can breakdown and reproduce for ourselves. The goal is to empower each willing individual to become the ultimate Captain of his or her destiny, and to do it, again and again. Welcome to the Alphas.

ALPHA LADDERS 2 -081
SHAPING LEADERS AND ACHIEVERS
BY Dr. BAK NGUYEN & BRENDA GARCIA

In ALPHA LADDERS 2, Dr. Bak is sharing the second part of his private conversation and board meetings with his trusted lieutenants. This time it is with international Counsellor, Brenda Garcia that the dialogue is taking place. In this second tome, the journey is taken to the next level. If the first tome was about the WHYs and the HOWs at an individual level, this tome is about the WHYs and the HOWs at the societal level. Through the lens of her background in international relations and diplomacy, Brenda now has the mission to help Dr. Bak establish structures, not only for his emerging organization and legacy, THE ALPHAS, but to also inspire all the other leaders and structures of our society. To do this, Brenda is taking Dr. Bak on an anthropological, sociological and philosophical journey to revisit different historical key moments in various fields and eras, going as far back as in ancient Greece at the dawn of democracy, all the way to the golden era of modern multilateralism embodied by the UN structure. Learning from the legacies of prominent figures going from Plato to Ban Ki Moon, Martin Luther King or Nelson Mandela, to Machiavelli, Marx and Simone de Beauvoir, Brenda and Dr. Bak are attempting to grasp the essence of structure and hierarchy, their goal being to empower each willing individual to become the ultimate Captain of their own success, to climb up the ladders no matter how high it is, and to build their legacy one step at a time.

AMONGST THE ALPHAS -058
BY Dr. BAK NGUYEN, with Dr. MARIA KUNDSTATER, Dr. PAUL OUELLETTE and Dr. JEREMY KRELL

In AMONGST THE ALPHAS Dr. Bak opens the blueprint of the next level with the hope that everyone can be better, bigger, wiser, but above all, a philosophy of Life that if, well applied, can bring inspiration to life. The Alphas rose in the midst of the COVID war as an International Collaboration to empower individuals to rise from the global crisis. Joining Dr. Bak are some of the world thinkers and achievers, the Alphas. Doctors, business people, thinkers, achievers, influencers, they are coming together to define what is an Alpha and his or her role, making the world a better place. This isn't the American dream, it is the human dream, one that can help you make History. Joining Dr. Bak are 3 Alpha authors, Dr. Maria Kundstater, Dr. Paul Ouellette and Dr. Jeremy Krell. This book started with questions from coach Jonas Diop. Welcome to the Alphas.

AMONGST THE ALPHAS vol.2 -059
ON THE OTHER SIDE
BY Dr. BAK NGUYEN with Dr. JULIO REYNAFARJE, Dr. LINA DUSEVICIUTE and Dr. DUC-MINH LAM-DO

In AMONGST THE ALPHAS 2, Dr. Bak continues to explore the meaning of what it is to be an Alpha and how to act amongst Alphas, because as the saying taught us: alone one goes fast, together we goes far. Some people see the problem. Some people look at the problem, some people created the problem. Some people leverage the problem into solutions and opportunities. Well, all of those people are Alphas. Networking and leveraging one another, their powers and reach are beyond measure. And one will keep the other in line too. Joining Dr. Bak are 3 Alphas from around the world coming together to share and collaborate, Dr. DUSEVICIUTE, Dr. LAM-DO and Dr. REYNAFARJE. This isn't the American dream, it is the human dream, one that can help you make History. Welcome to the Alphas.

B

BOOTCAMP -071
BOOKS TO REWRITE MINDSETS INTO WINNING STATES OF MIND
BY Dr. BAK NGUYEN

In BOOTCAMP 8 BOOKS TO REWRITE MINDSETS INTO WINNING STATES OF MIND, Dr. Bak is taking you into his past, before the visionary entrepreneur, before the world records, before the Industry's disruptor status. Here are 8 of the books that changed Dr. Bak's thinking and, therefore, reset his evolution into the course we now know him for. BOOTCAMP: 8 BOOKS TO REWRITE MINDSETS INTO WINNING STATES OF MIND, is a Bootcamp of 8 weeks for anyone looking to experience Dr. Bak's training to become THE Dr. BAK you came to know and love. This book will summarize how each title changed Dr. Bak mindset into a state of mind and how he applied that to rewrite his destiny. 8 books to read, that's 8 weeks of Bootcamp to access the power of your MIND and of your WILL. Are you ready for a change?

BRANDING -044
BALANCING STRATEGY AND EMOTIONS
BY Dr. BAK NGUYEN

BRANDING is communication to its most powerful state. Branding is not just about communicating anymore but about making a promise, about establishing a relation, about generating an emotion. More than once, Dr. Bak proved himself to be a master, communicating and branding his ideas into flags attracting interest and influences, nationally and internationally. In BRANDING, Dr. Bak shares a very unique and personal journey, branding Dr. Bak. How does he go from Dr. Nguyen, a loved and respected dentist to becoming Dr. Bak, a world anchor hosting THE ALPHAS in the medical and financial world?More than a personal journey, BRANDING helps to break down the steps to elevate someone with nothing else but the force of his or her spirit. Welcome to the Alphas.

C

CHANGING THE WORLD FROM A DENTAL CHAIR -007
BY Dr. BAK NGUYEN

Since he has received the EY's nomination for entrepreneur of the year for his startup Mdex & Co, Dr. Bak Nguyen has pushed the opportunity to the next level. Speaker, author, and businessman, Dr. Bak is a true entrepreneur and industries' disruptor. To compensate for the startup's status of Mdex & Co, he challenged himself to write a book based on the EY's questionnaire to share an in-depth vision of his company. With "Changing the World from a dental chair" Dr. Bak is sharing his thought process and philosophy to his approach to the industry. Not looking to revolutionize but rather to empower, he became, despite himself, an industries disruptor: an entrepreneur who has established a new benchmark. Dr. Bak Nguyen is a cosmetic dentist and visionary businessman who won the GRAND HOMAGE prize of "LYS de la Diversité" 2016, for his contribution as a citizen and entrepreneur in the community. He also holds recognitions from the Canadian Parliament and the Canadian Senate.

In 2003, he founded Mdex, a dental company upon which in 2018, he launched the most ambitious private endeavour to reform the dental industry, Canada wide. He wrote seven books covering ENTREPRENEURSHIP, LEADERSHIP, QUEST of IDENTITY, and now, PROFESSION HEALTH. Philosopher, he has close to his heart the quest of happiness of the people surrounding him, patients, and colleagues alike. Those projects have allowed Dr. Nguyen to attract interests from the international and diplomatic community and he is now the centre of a global discussion on the wellbeing and the future of the health profession. It is in that matter that he shares with you his thoughts and encourages the health community to share their own stories.

CHAMPION MINDSET -039
LEARNING TO WIN
BY Dr. BAK NGUYEN & CHRISTOPHE MULUMBA

CHAMPION MINDSET is the encounter of the business world and the professional sports world. Industries' Disruptor Dr. BAK NGUYEN shares his wisdom and views with the HAMMER, CFL Football Star, Edmonton's Eskimos CHRISTOPHE MULUMBA on how to leverage on the champion mindset to create successful entrepreneurs. Writing and challenging each other, they discovered the parallels and the difference of both worlds, but mainly, the recipe for leveraging from one to succeed in the other, from champions and entrepreneurs to WINNERS. Build and score your millions, it is a matter of mindset! This is CHAMPION MINDSET.

E

EMPOWERMENT -069
BY Dr. BAK NGUYEN

In EMPOWERMENT, Dr. Bak's 69th book, writing a book every 8 days for 8 weeks in a row to write the next world record of writing 72 books/36 months, Dr. Bak is taking a rest, sharing his inner feelings, inspiration, and motivation. Much more than his dairy, EMPOWERMENT is the key to walk in his footsteps and to comprehend the process of an overachiever. Dr. Bak's helped and inspired countless people to find their voice, to live their dream, and to be the better version of themselves. Why is he sharing as much and keep sharing? Why is he going that fast, always further and further, why and how is he keeping his inspiration and momentum? Those are all the answers EMPOWERMENT will deliver to you. This book might be one of the fastest Dr. Bak has written, not because of time constraints but from inspiration, pure inspiration to share and to grow. There is always a dark side to each power, two faces to a coin. Well, this is the less prominent facets of Dr. Bak Momentum and success, the road to his MINDSET.

F

FORCES OF NATURE -015
FORGING THE CHARACTER OF WINNERS
BY Dr. BAK NGUYEN

In FORCES OF NATURE, Dr. Bak is giving his all. This is his 15 books written within 15 months. It is the end of a marathon to set the next world record. For the occasion, he wanted to end with a big bang! How about a book with all of his biggest challenges? A Quest of Identity, a journey looking for his name and powers, Dr. Bak is borrowing with myths and legends to make this journey universal. Yes, this is Dr. Bak's mythology. Demons, heroes and Gods, there are forces of Nature that we all meet on our way for our name. Some will scare us, some will fight us, some will manipulate us. We can flee, we can hide, we can fight. What we do will define our next encounter and the one after. A tale of personal growth, a journey to find power and purpose, Dr. Bak is showing us the path to freedom, the Path of Life. Welcome to the Alphas.

H

HORIZON, BUILDING UP THE VISION -045
VOLUME ONE
BY Dr. BAK NGUYEN

Dr. Bak is opening up at your demand! Many of you are following Dr. Bak online and are asking to know more about his lifestyle. This is how he has chosen to respond: sharing his lifestyle as he traveled the world and what he learned in each city to come to build his Mindset as a driver and a winner. Here are 10 destinations (over 69 that will be following in the next volumes...) in which he shares his journey. New York, Quebec, Paris, Punta Cana, Monaco, Los Angeles, Nice, Holguin, the journey happened over twenty years.

HORIZON, ON THE FOOTSTEP OF TITANS -048
VOLUME TWO
BY Dr. BAK NGUYEN

Dr. Bak is opening up at your demand! Many of you are following Dr. Bak online and are asking to know more about his lifestyle. This is how he has chosen to respond: sharing his lifestyle as he traveled the world and what he learned in each city to come to build his Mindset as a driver and a winner. Here are 9 destinations (over 72 that will be following in the next volumes...) in which he shares his journey. Hong Kong, London, Rome, San Francisco, Anaheim, and more..., the journey happened over twenty years. Dr. Bak is sharing with you his feelings, impressions, and how they shaped his state of mind and character into Dr. Bak. From a dreamer to a driver and a builder, the journey started since he was 3. Wealth is a state of mind, and a state of mind is the basis of the drive. Find out about the mind of an Industry's disruptor.

HORIZON, Dr.EAMING OF THE FUTURE -068
VOLUME THREE
BY Dr. BAK NGUYEN

Dr. Bak is back. From the midst of confinement, he remembers and writes about what life was, when traveling was a natural part of Life. It will come back. Now more than ever, we need to open both our hearts and minds to fight fear and intolerance. Writing from a time of crisis, he is sharing the magic and psychological effect of seeing the world and how it has shaped his mindset. Here are 9 other destinations (over 75) in which he shares his journey. Beijing, Key West, Madrid, Amsterdam, Marrakech and more..., the journey happened over twenty years.

HOW TO NOT FAIL AS A DENTIST -047
BY Dr. BAK NGUYEN

In HOW TO NOT FAIL AS A DENTIST, Dr. Bak is given 20 plus years of experience and knowledge of what it is to be a dentist on the ground. PROFESSIONAL INTELLIGENCE, FINANCIAL INTELLIGENCE and MANAGEMENT INTELLIGENCE are the fields that any dentist will have to master for a chance to success and a shot for happiness practicing dentistry. Where ever you are starting your career as a new graduate or a veteran in the field looking to reach the next level, this is book smart and street smart all into one. This is Million Dollar Mindset applied to dentistry. We won't be making a millionaire out of you from this book, we will be giving you a shot to happiness and success. The million will follow soon enough.

HOW TO WRITE A BOOK IN 30 DAYS -042
BY Dr. BAK NGUYEN

In HOW TO WRITE YOUR BOOK IN 30 DAYS, Dr. Bak has crafted writing skills and techniques that can be shared and mastered. This book is mainly about structure and how to keep moving forward, avoiding the hit of the INSPIRATION WALL. You will find a wealth of wisdom from his experience writing your first, second, or even 10th book. Dr. Bak is sharing his secrets writing books, having written himself 72 books within 36 months. Visionary businessman, doctor in dentistry, Dr. Bak describes himself as a Dentist by circumstances, a communicator by passion, and an entrepreneur by nature.

HOW TO WRITE A SUCCESSFUL BUSINESS PLAN -049
BY Dr. BAK NGUYEN & ROUBA SAKR

In HOW TO WRITE A SUCCESSFUL BUSINESS PLAN, Dr. Bak is given 20 plus years of experience and knowledge of what it is to be an entrepreneur and more importantly, how to have the investors and banks on your side. Being an entrepreneur is surely not something you learn from school, but there are steps to master so you can communicate your views and vision. That's the only way you will have financing.Writing a business is only not a mandatory stop only for the bankers, but an essential step to every entrepreneur, to know the direction and what's coming next. A business plan is also not set in stone, if there is a truth in business is that nothing will go as planned. Writing down your business plan the first time will prepare you to adapt and to overcome the challenges and surprises. For most entrepreneurs, a business is a passion. To most investors and all banks, a business is a system. Your business plan is the map to that system. However unique your ideas and business are, the mapping follows the same steps and pattern.

HUMILITY FOR SUCCESS -051
BALANCING STRATEGY AND EMOTIONS
BY Dr. BAK NGUYEN

HUMILITY FOR SUCCESS is exploring the emotional discomforts and challenges champions, and overachievers put themselves through. Success is never done overnight and on the way, just like the pain and the struggles aren't enough, we are dealing with the doubts, the haters, and those who like to tell us how to live our lives and what to do. At the same time, nothing of worth can be achieved alone. Every legend has a cast of characters, allies, mentors, companions, rivals, and foes. So one needs the key to social behaviour. HUMILITY FOR SUCCESS is exploring the matter and will help you sort out beliefs from values, peers from friends. Humility is much more about how we see ourselves than how others see us. For any entrepreneur and champion, our daily is to set our mindset right, and to perfect our skills, not to fit in. There is a world where CONFIDENCE grows is in synergy with HUMILITY. As you set the right label on the right belief, you will be able to grow and to leave the lies and haters far behinds. This is HUMILITY FOR SUCCESS.

HYBRID -011
THE MODERN QUEST OF IDENTITY
BY Dr. BAK NGUYEN

IDENTITY -004
THE ANTHOLOGY OF QUESTS
BY Dr. BAK NGUYEN

What if John Lennon was still alive and running for president today? What kind of campaign will he be running? IDENTIFY -THE ANTHOLOGY OF QUESTS is about the quest each of us has to undertake, sooner or later, THE QUEST OF IDENTITY. Citizen of the world, aim to be one, the one, one whole, one unity, made of many. That's the anthology of life! Start with your one, find your unity, and your legend will start. We are all small-minded people anyway! We need each other to be one! We need each other to be happy, so we, so you, so I, can be happy. This is the chorus of life. This is our song! Citizens of the world, I salute you! This is the first tome of the IDENTITY QUEST. FORCES OF NATURE (tome 2) will be following in SUMMER 2021. Also under development, Tome 3 - THE CONQUEROR WITHIN will start production soon.

INDUSTRIES DISRUPTORS -006
BY Dr. BAK NGUYEN

INDUSTRIES DISRUPTORS is a strange title, one that sparkles mixed feelings. A disruptor is someone making a difference, and since we, in general, do not like change, the label is mostly negative. But a disruptor is mostly someone who sees the same problem and challenge from another angle. The disruptor will tackle that angle and come up with something new from something existent. That's evolution! In INDUSTRIES DISRUPTORS, Dr. Bak is joining forces with James Stephan-Usypchuk to share with us what is going on in the minds and shoes of those entrepreneurs disrupting the old habits. Dr. Bak is changing the world from a dental chair, disrupting the dental, and now the book industry. James is a maverick in the Intelligence space, from marketing to Artificial Intelligence. Coming from very different backgrounds and industries, they end up telling very similar stories. If disruptors change the world, well, their story proves that disruptors can be made and forged. Here's the recipe. Here are their stories.

K

KRYPTO -040
TO SAVE THE WORLD
BY Dr. BAK NGUYEN & ILYAS BAKOUCH

L

LEADERSHIP -003
PANDORA'S BOX
BY Dr. BAK NGUYEN

LEADERSHIP, PANDORA'S BOX is 21 presidential speeches for a better tomorrow for all of us. It aims to drive HOPE and motivation into each and every one of us. Together we can make the difference, we hold such power. Covering themes from LOYALTY to GENEROSITY, from FREEDOM and INTELLIGENCE to DOUBTS and DEATH, this is not the typical presidential or motivational speeches that we are used to. LEADERSHIP PANDORA'S BOX will surf your emotions first, only to dive with you to touch the core and soul of our meaning: to matter. This is not a Quest of Identity, but the cry to rally as a species, to raise our heads toward the future, and to move forward as a WHOLE. Not a typical Dr. Bak's book, LEADERSHIP, PANDORA'S BOX is a must-read for all of you looking for hope and purpose, all of us, citizens of the world.

LEVERAGE -014
COMMUNICATION INTO SUCCESS

BY Dr. BAK NGUYEN

In LEVERAGE COMMUNICATION TO SUCCESS, Dr. Bak shares his secret and mindsets to elevate an idea into a vision and a vision into an endeavour. Some endeavours will be a project, some others will become companies, and some will grow into a movement. It does not matter, each started with great communication.Communication is a very vast concept, education, sale, sharing, empowering, coaching, preaching, entertaining. Those are all different kinds of communication. The intent differs, the audiences vary, the messages are unique but the frame can be templated and mastered. In LEVERAGE COMMUNICATION TO SUCCESS, Dr. Bak is loyal to his core, sharing only what he knows best, what he has done himself. This book is dedicated to communicating successfully in business.

M

MASTERMIND, 7 WAYS INTO THE BIG LEAGUE -052
BY Dr. BAK NGUYEN & JONAS DIOP

MASTERMIND, 7 WAYS INTO THE BIG LEAGUE is the result of the encounter of business coach Jonas Diop and Dr. Bak. As a professional podcaster and someone always seeking the truth and ways to leverage success and performance, coach Jonas is putting Dr. Bak to the test, one that should reveal his secret to overachieve month after month, accumulating a new world record every month. Follow those two great minds as they push each other to surpass themselves, each in their own way and own style. MASTERMIND, 7 WAYS INTO THE BIG LEAGUE is more than a roadmap to success, it is a journey and a live testimony as you are turning the pages, one by one.

MIDAS TOUCH -065
POST-COVID DENTISTRY
BY Dr. BAK NGUYEN, Dr. JULIO REYNAFARJE AND Dr. PAUL OUELLETTE

MIDAS TOUCH, is the memoir of what happened in the ALPHAS SUMMIT in the midst of the GREAT PAUSE as great minds throughout the world in the dental field are coming together. As the time of competition is obsolete, the new era of collaboration is blooming. This is the 3rd book of the ALPHAS, after AFTERMATH and RELEVANCY, all written in the midst of confinement. Dr. Julio Reynafarje is bearing this initiative, to share with you the secret of a successful and lasting relationship with your patients, balancing science and psychology, kindness, and professionalism. He personally invited the ALPHAS to join as co-author, Dr. Paul Ouellette, and Dr. Paul Dominique, and Dr. Bak.Together, they have more than 100 years of combined experience, wisdom, trade, skills, philosophy, and secrets to share with you to empower you in the rebuilding of the dental profession in the aftermath of COVID. RELEVANCY was about coming together and to rebuild the future. MIDAS TOUCH is about how to build, one treatment plan at a time, one story at a time, one smile at a time.

MINDSET ARMORY -050
BY Dr. BAK NGUYEN

MINDSET ARMORY is Dr. Bak's 49th book, days after he completed his world record of writing 48 books within 24 months, on top of being a CEO of Mdex & Co and a full-time cosmetic dentist. Dr. Bak is undoubtedly an OVERACHIEVER. From his last books, he has shared more and more of his lifestyle and how it forged his winning mindset. Within MINDSET ARMORY, Dr. Bak is sharing with us his tools, how he found them, forged them, and leverage them. Just like any warrior needs a shield, a sword, and a ride, here are Dr. Bak's. For any entrepreneur, the road to success is a long and winding journey. On the way, some will find allies and foes. Some allies will become foes, and some foes might become allies. In today's competitive world, the only constant is change. With the right tool, it is possible to achieve. The right tool, the right mindset. This is MINDSET ARMORY.

MIRROR -085
BY Dr. BAK NGUYEN

MIRROR is the theme for a personal book. Not only to Dr. Bak but to all of us looking to reach beyond who and what we actually are. MIRROR is special in the fact that it is not only the content of the book that is of worth but the process in which Dr. Bak shared his own evolution. To go beyond who we are, one must grow every day. And how do you compare your growth and how far have you reach? Looking in the mirror. In all of Dr. Bak's writing, looking at the past is a trap to avoid at all costs. Looking in the mirror, is that any better? Share Dr. Bak's way to push and keep pushing himself without friction nor resistance. Please read that again. To evolve without friction or resistance... that is the source of infinite growth and the unification of the Quest for Power and the Quest of Happiness.

MOMENTUM TRANSFER -009
BY Dr. BAK NGUYEN & Coach DINO MASSON

How to be successful in your business and in your life? Achieve Your Biggest Goals With MOMENTUM TRANSFER. START THE BUSINESS YOU WANT - AND BRING IT NEXT LEVEL! GET THE LIFE YOU ALWAYS WANTED - AND IMPROVE IT! TAKE ANY PROJECTS YOU HAVE - AND MAKE IT THE BEST! In this powerful book, you'll discover what a small business owner learned from a millionaire and successful entrepreneur. He applied his mentor's principles and is explaining them in full detail in this book. The small business owner wrote the book he has always wanted to read and went from the verge of bankruptcy to quadrupling his revenues in less than 9 months and improve his personal life by increasing his energy and bring back peacefulness. Together, the millionaire and the small business owner are sharing their most valuable business and life lessons to the world. The most powerful book to increase your momentum in your business and your life introduces simple and radical life-changing concepts: Multiply your business revenues by finding the Eye of your Momentum - Increase your energy by building and feeding your own Momentum - How to increase your confidence with these simple steps - How to transfer your new powerful energy into other aspects of your business and life - How to set goals and achieve them (even crush them!)- How to always tap into an effortless and limitless force within you- And much, much more!

P

PLAYBOOK INTRODUCTION -055
BY Dr. BAK NGUYEN

In PLAYBOOK INTRODUCTION, Dr. Bak is open the door to all the newcomers and aspirant entrepreneurs who are looking at where and when to start. Based on questions of two college students wanting to know how to start their entrepreneurial journey, Dr. Bak dives into his experiences to empower the next generation, not about what they should do, but how he, Dr. Bak, would have done it today. This is an important aspect to recognize in the business world, the world has changed since the INFORMATION AGE and the advent of the millenniums into the market. Most matrix and know-how have to be adapted to today's speed and accessibility to the information. We are living at the INFORMATION AGE, this book is the precursor to the ABUNDANCE AGE, at least to those open to embrace the opportunity.

PLAYBOOK INTRODUCTION 2 -056
BY Dr. BAK NGUYEN

In PLAYBOOK INTRODUCTION 2, Dr. Bak continuing the journey to welcome the newcomers and aspirant entrepreneurs looking at where and when to start. If the first volume covers the mindset, the second is covering much more in-depth the concept of debt and leverage.This is an important aspect to recognize in the business world, the world has changed since the INFORMATION AGE and the advent of the millenniums into the market. Most matrix and know-how have to be adapted to today's speed and accessibility to the information. We are living at the INFORMATION AGE, this book is the precursor to the ABUNDANCE AGE, at least to those open to embrace the opportunity.

POWER -043
EMOTIONAL INTELLIGENCE
BY Dr. BAK NGUYEN

IN POWER, EMOTIONAL INTELLIGENCE, Dr. Bak is sharing his experiences and secrets leveraging on his EMOTIONAL INTELLIGENCE, a power we all have within. From SYMPATHY, having others opening up to you, to ACTIVE LISTENING, saving you time and energy; from EMPATHY, allowing you to predict the future to INFLUENCE, enabling you to draft the future, not to forget the power of the crowd with MOMENTUM, you are now in possession of power in tune with nature, yourself. It is a unique take on the subject to empower you to find your powers and your destiny. Visionary businessman, doctor in dentistry, Dr. Bak describes himself as a Dentist by circumstances, a communicator by passion, and an entrepreneur by nature.

POWERPLAY -078
HOW TO BUILD THE PERFECT TEAM
BY Dr. BAK NGUYEN

In POWERPLAY, HOW TO BUILD THE PERFECT TEAM, Dr. Bak is sharing with you his experience, perspective, and mistake traveling the journey of the entrepreneur. A serial entrepreneur himself, he started venture only with a single partner as team to build companies with a director of human resources and a board of directors. POWERPLAY is not a story, it is the HOW TO build the perfect team, knowing that perfection is a lie. So how can one build a team that will empower his or her vision? How to recruit, how to train, how to retain? Those are all legitimate questions. And all of those won't matter if the first question isn't answered: what is the reason for the team? There is the old way to hire and the new way to recruit. Yes, Human Resources is all about mindset too! This journey is one of introspection, of leadership, and a cheat sheet to build, not only the perfect team but the team that will empower your legacy to the next level.

PROFESSION HEALTH - TOME ONE -005
THE UNCONVENTIONAL QUEST OF HAPPINESS
BY Dr. BAK NGUYEN, Dr. MIRJANA SINDOLIC, Dr. ROBERT DURAND AND COLLABORATORS

Why are health professionals burning out while they give the best of themselves to heal the world? Dr. Bak aims to break the curse of isolation that health professionals face and establish a conversation to start the healing process. PROFESSION HEALTH is the basis of an ongoing discussion and will also serve as an introduction to a study lead by Professor Robert Durand, DMD, MSc Science from University of Montreal, study co-financed by Mdex and the Federal Government of Canada. Co-writers are Dr. Mirjana Sindolic, Professor Robert Durand, Dr. Jean De Serres, MD and former President of Hema Quebec, Counsel-Minister Luis Maria Kalaff Sanchez, Dr. Miguel Angel Russo, MD, Banker Anthony Siggia, Banker Kyles Yves, and more...
This is the first Tome of three, dedicated to help "WHITE COATS" to heal and to find their happiness.

R

REBOOT -012
MIDLIFE CRISIS
BY Dr. BAK NGUYEN

MidLife Crisis is a common theme to each of us as we reach the threshold. As a man, as a woman, why is it that half of the marriages end up in recall? If anything else would have half those rates of failure, the lawsuits would be raining. Where are the flaws, the traps? Love is strong and pure, why is marriage not the reflection of that?

All hard to ask questions with little or no answers. Dr. Bak is sharing his reflections and findings as he reached himself the WALL OF MARRIAGE. This is a matter that affects all of our lives. It is time for some answers.

RELEVANCY - TOME TWO -064
REINVENTING OURSELVES TO SURVIVE
BY Dr. BAK NGUYEN & Dr. PAUL OUELLETTE AND COLLABORATORS

THE GREAT PAUSE was a reboot of all the systems of society. Many outdated systems will not make it back. The Dental Industry is a needed one, it has laid on complacency for far too long. In an age where expertise is global and democratized and can be replaced with technologies and artificial intelligence, the REBOOT will force, not just an update, but an operating system replacement and a firmware upgrade.First, they saved their industry with THE ALPHAS INITIATIVE, sharing their knowledge and vision freely to all the world's dental industry. With the OUELLETTE INITIATIVE, they bought some time to all the dental clinics to resume and to adjust. The warning has been given, the clock is now ticking. who will prevail and prosper and who will be left behind, outdated and obsolete?

RISING -062
TO WIN MORE THAN YOU ARE AFRAID TO LOSE
BY Dr. BAK NGUYEN

In RISING, TO WIN MORE TAN YOU ARE AFRAID TO LOSE, Dr. Bak is breaking down the strategy to success to all, not only those wearing white coats and scrubs. More than his previous book (SUCCESS IS A CHOICE), this one is covering most of the aspects of getting to the next level, psychologically, socially, and financially. Rising is broken down into three key strategies: Financial Leverage - Compressing time - Always being in control. Presented by MILLION DOLLAR MINDSET, the book is covering more than the ways to create wealth, but also how to reach happiness and to live a life without regrets. Dr. Bak the CEO and founder of Mdex & Co, a company with the promise of reforming the whole dental industry for the better. He wrote more than 60 books within 30 months as he is sharing his experiences, secrets, and wisdom.

S

SELFMADE -036
GRATITUDE AND HUMILITY
BY Dr. BAK NGUYEN

This is the story of Dr. Bak, an artist who became a dentist, a dentist who became an Entrepreneur, an Entrepreneur who is seeking to save an entire industry.In his free time, Dr. Bak managed to write 37 books and is a contender to 3 world records to be confirmed. Businessman and visionary, his views and philosophy are ahead of our time. This is his 37th book. In SELFMADE, Dr. Bak is answering the questions most entrepreneurs want to know, the HOWTO and the secret recipes, not just to succeed, but to keep going no matter what! SELFMADE is the perfect read for any entrepreneurs, novices, and veterans.

SUCCESS IS A CHOICE -060
BLUEPRINTS FOR HEALTH PROFESSIONALS
BY Dr. BAK NGUYEN

In SUCCESS IS A CHOICE, FINANCIAL MILLIONAIRE BLUEPRINTS FOR HEALTH PROFESSIONALS, Dr. Bak is breaking down the strategy to success for all those wearing white coats and scrubs: doctors, dentists, pharmacists, chiropractors, nurses, etc. Success is broken down into three key strategies: Financial Leverage - Compressing time - Always being in control. Presented by MILLION DOLLAR MINDSET, the book is covering more than the ways to create wealth, but also how to reach happiness and to live a life without regrets.Dr. Bak is a successful cosmetic dentist with nearly 20 years of experience. He founded Mdex & Co, a company with the promise of reforming the whole dental industry for the better. While doing so, he discovered a passion for writing and for sharing. Multiple times World Record, Dr. Bak is writing a book every 2 weeks for the last 30 months. This is his 60th book, and he is still practicing. How he does it, is what he is sharing with us, SUCCESS, HAPPINESS, and mostly FREEDOM to all Health Professionals.

SYMPHONY OF SKILLS -001
BY Dr. BAK NGUYEN

You will enlighten the world with your potential. I can't wait to see all the differences that you will have in our world. Remember that power comes with responsibility. We can feel in his presence, a genuine force, a depth of energy, confidence, innocence, courage, and intelligence. Bak is always looking for answers, morning and night, he wants to understand the why and the why not. This book is the essence of the man. Dr. Bak is a force of nature who bears proudly his title eHappy. The man never ceases smiling nor spreading his good vibe wherever he passes. He is not trapped in the nostalgia of the past nor the satisfaction of the present, he embodies the joy of what's possible, what's to come. The more we read, the more we share, and we live. That is Bak, he charms us to evolve and to share his points of view, and before we know it, we are walking by his side, a journey we never saw coming.

T

THE 90 DAYS CHALLENGE -061
BY Dr. BAK NGUYEN

THE 90 DAYS CHALLENGE, is Dr. Bak's journey into the unknown. Overachiever writing 2 books a month on average, for the last 30 months, ambitious CEO, Industries' Disruptor, Dr. Bak seems to have success in everything he touches. Everything except the control of his weight. For nearly 20 years, he struggles with an overweight problem. Every time he scored big, he added on a little more weight. Well, this time, he exposes himself out there, in real-time and without filter, accepting the challenge of his brother-in-law, DON VO to lose 45 pounds within 90 days. That's half a pound a day, for three months. He will have to do so while keeping all of his other challenges on track, writing books at a world record pace, leading the dental industry into the new ERA, and keep seeing his patients. Undoubtedly entertaining, this is the journey of an ALPHA who simply won't give up. But this time, nothing is sure.

THE BOOK OF LEGENDS -024
BY Dr. BAK NGUYEN & WILLIAM BAK

The Book of Legends vol. 1 the story behind the world record of Dr. Bak and his son, William Bak. All Dr. Bak had in mind was to keep his promise of writing a book with his son. They ended up writing 8 children's books within a month, scoring a new world record. William is also the youngest author having published in two languages. Those are world records waiting to be confirmed. History will say: to celebrate a first world record (writing 15 books / 15 months), for the love of his son, he will have scored a second world record: to write 8 books within a month! THE BOOK OF LEGENDS vol. 1 This is both a magical journey for both a father and a son looking to connect and to find themselves. Join Dr. Bak and William Bak in their journey and their love for Life!

THE BOOK OF LEGENDS 2 -041
BY Dr. BAK NGUYEN & WILLIAM BAK

THE BOOK OF LEGENDS vol. 2 is the sequel of "CINDERELLA" but a true story between a father and his son. Together they have discovered a bond and a way to connect. The first BOOK OF LEGENDS covered the time of the first four books they wrote together within a month. The second BOOK OF LEGENDS is covering what happened after the curtains dropped, what happened after reality kicked back in. If the first volume was about a fairy tale in vacation time, the second volume is about making it last in real Life. Share their journey and their love of Life!

THE BOOK OF LEGENDS 3 -086
THE END OF THE INNOCENCE AGE
BY Dr. BAK NGUYEN & WILLIAM BAK

This is the third volume of the series, THE BOOK OF LEGENDS. If the first two happened as a breeze breaking world records on top of world records (27 books written as father and son), the 3rd volume took much more time to arrive. William has grown and writing chicken books is not enough anymore to ignite his imagination. Dr. Bak, as a good father, will try to follow William's growth and invented new games, technics and mind frames to keep engaging William's imagination and interest. From auditions to backstories, Dr. Bak bent backward to keep the adventure going. More than sharing the success and the glory, within THE BOOK OF LEGENDS volume 3, you are sharing the doubts and failure of a father and son refusing to let go... but who have now left MOMENTUM... until the winds blow once more in their favour. Welcome to the Alphas.

THE CONFESSION OF A LAZY OVERACHIEVER -089
REINVENT YOURSELF FROM ANY CRISIS
BY Dr. BAK NGUYEN

In THE CONFESSION OF A LAZY OVERACHIEVER, Dr. Bak is opening up to his new marketing officer, Jamie, fresh out of school. She is young, full of energy, and looking to chill and still to have it all. True to his character, Dr. Bak is giving Jamie some leeway to redefine Dr. Bak's brand to her demographic, the Millennials. This journey is about Dr. Bak satisfying the Millennials and answering their true questions in life. A rebel himself, his ambition to change the world started back on campus, some 25 years ago... then, life caught up with him. It took Dr. Bak 20 years to shake down the burdens of life, to spread his wings free from Conformity, and to start Overachieving. Doctor, CEO, and world record author, here is what Dr. Bak would have love to know 25 years ago as was still on campus. In a word, this is cheating your way to success and freedom. And yes, it is possible. Success, Money, Freedom, it all starts with a mindset and the awareness of Time. Welcome to the Alphas.

THE ENERGY FORMULA -053
BY Dr. BAK NGUYEN

THE ENERGY FORMULA is a book dedicated to help each individual to find the means to reach their purpose and goal in Life. Dr. Bak is a philosopher, a strategist, a business, an artist, and a dentist, how does he do all of that? He is doing so while mentoring proteges and leading the modernization of an entire industry. Until now, Momentum and Speed were the powers that he was building on and from. But those powers come from somewhere too. From a guide of our Quest of Identity, he became an ally in everyone's journey for happiness. THE ENERGY FORMULA is the book revealing step by step, the logic of building the right mindset and the way to ABUNDANCE and HAPPINESS, universally. It is not just a HOW TO book, but one that will change your life and guide you to the path of ABUNDANCE.

THE MODERN WOMAN -070
TO HAVE IT HAVE WITH NO SACRIFICE
BY Dr. BAK NGUYEN & Dr. EMILY LETRAN

In THE MODERN WOMAN: TO HAVE IT ALL WITH NO SACRIFICE, Dr. Bak joins forces with Dr. Emily Letran to empower all women to fulfill their desires, goals, and ambition. Both overachievers going against the odds, they are sharing their experience and wisdom to help all women to find confidence and support to redefine their lives. Dr. Emily Letran is a doctor in dentistry, an entrepreneur, author, and CERTIFIED HIGH-PERFORMANCE coach. For an Asian woman, she made it through the norms and the red tapes to find her voice. As she learned and grew with mentors, today she is sharing her secret with the energy that will motivate all of the female genders to stand for what they deserve. Alpha doctor, Bak is joining his voice and perspective since this is not about gender equality, but about personal empowerment and the quest of Identity of each, man and woman. Once more, Dr. Bak is bringing LEVERAGE and REASON to the new social deal between man and woman. This is not about gender, but about confidence.

THE POWER BEHIND THE ALPHA -008
BY TRANIE VO & Dr. BAK NGUYEN

It's been said by a "great man" that "We are born alone and we die alone." Both men and women proudly repeat those words as wisdom since. I apologize in advance, but what a fat LIE! That's what I learned and discovered in life since my mind and heart got liberated from the burden of scars and the ladders of society. I can have it all, not all at the same time, but I can have everything I put my mind and heart into. Actually, it is not completely true. I can have most of what I and Tranie put our minds into. Together, when we feel like one, there isn't much out of our reach. If I'm the mind, she's the heart; if I'm the Will, she's the means. Synergy is the core of our power.Tranie's aim is always Happiness. In Tranie's definition of life, there are no justifications, no excuses, no tomorrow. For Tranie, Happiness is measured by the minutes of every single day. This is why she's so strong and can heal people around her. That may also be why she doesn't need to talk much, since talking about the past or the future is, in her mind, dimming down the magic of the present, the Now. We both respect and appreciate that we are the whole balancing each other's equation of life, of love, of success. I was the plus and the minus, then I became the multiplication factor and grew into the exponential. And how is Tranie evolving in all of this? She is and always will be the balance. If anything, she is the equal sign of each equation.

THE POWER OF Dr. -066
THE MODERN TITLE OF NOBILITY
BY Dr. BAK NGUYEN, Dr. PAVEL KRASTEV AND COLLABORATORS

In THE POWER OF Dr., independent thinkers mean to exchange ideas. An idea can be very powerful if supported with a great work ethic. Work ethic, isn't that the main fabric of our white coats, scrubs, and title? In an era post-COVID where everything has been rebooted and that the healthcare industry is facing its own fate: to evolve or to be replaced, Dr. Bak and Dr. Pavel reveal the source of their power and their playbook to move forward, ahead.The power we all hold is our resilience and discipline. We put that for years at the service of our profession, from a surgical perspective. Now, we can harness that same power to rewrite the rules, the industry, and our future. Post-COVID, the rules are being rewritten, will you be part of the team or left behind?
"You can be in control!" More than personal growth and a motivational book, THE POWER OF Dr. is an awakening call to the doctor you look at when you graduate, with hope, with honour, with determination.

THE POWER OF YES -010
VOLUME ONE: IMPACT
BY Dr. BAK NGUYEN

In THE POWER OF YES, Dr. Bak is sharing his journey opening up and embracing the world, one day at a time, one ask at a time, one wish at a time. Far from a dare, saying YES allowed Dr. Bak to rewrite his mindsets and to break all the boundaries. This book is not one written a few days or weeks, but the accumulation of a journey for 12 months. The journeys started as Dr. Bak said YES to his producer to go on stage and to speak... That YES opened a world of possibilities. Dr. Bak embraced each and every one of them. 12 months later, he is celebrating the new world record of writing 9 books written over a period of 12 months. To him, it will be a miss, missing the 12 on 12 mark. To the rest of the world, they just saw the birth of a force of nature, the Alpha force. THE POWER OF YES is comprised of all the introduction of the adult books written by Dr. Bak within the first 12 months. Chapter by chapter, you can walk in his footstep seeing and smelling what he has. This is reality literature with a twist of POWER. THE POWER OF YES! Discover your potential and your power. This is the POWER OF YES, volume one. Welcome to the Alphas.

THE POWER OF YES 2 -037
VOLUME TWO: SHAPELESS
BY Dr. BAK NGUYEN

In THE POWER OF YES, volume 2, Dr. Bak is continuing his journey discovering his powers and influence. After 12 months embracing the world saying YES, he rose as an emerging force: he's been recognized as an INDUSTRIES DISRUPTOR, got nominated ERNST AND YOUNG ENTREPRENEUR OF THE YEAR, wrote 9 books within 12 months while launching the most ambitious private endeavour to reform his own industry, the dental field. Contender too many WORLD RECORDS, Dr. Bak is doing all of that in parallel. And yes, he is sleeping his nights and yes, he is writing his book himself, from the screen of his iPhone! Far from satisfied, Dr. Bak missed the mark of writing 12 books within 12 months and everything else is shaping and moving, and could come crumbling down at each turn. Now that Dr. Bak understands his powers, he is looking to test them and to push them to their limits, looking to keep scoring world records while materializing his vision and enterprises. This is the awakening of a Force of Nature looking to change the world for the better while having fun sharing. Welcome to the Alphas.

THE POWER OF YES 3 -046
VOLUME THREE: LIMITLESS
BY Dr. BAK NGUYEN

In THE POWER OF YES, volume 3, the journey of Dr. Bak continues where the last volume left, in front of 300 plus people showing up to his first solo event, a Dr. Bak's event. On stage and in this book, Dr. Bak reveals how 12 months saying YES to everything changed his life... actually, it was 18 months.
From a dentist looking to change the world from a dental chair into a multiple times world record author, the journey of openness is a rendez-vous with Fate. Dr. Bak is sharing almost in real-time his journey, experiences, but above all, his feelings, doubts, and comebacks. From one book to the next, from one journey to the next, follow the adventure of a man looking to find his name, his worth, and his place in the world. Doing so, he is touching people Doing so, he is touching people and initiating their rises. Are you ready for more? Are you ready to meet your Fate and Destiny? Welcome to the Alphas.

THE POWER OF YES 4 -087
VOLUME FOUR: PURPOSE
BY Dr. BAK NGUYEN

In THE POWER OF YES, volume 4, the journey continues days after where the last volume left. After setting the new world record of writing 48 books within 24 months, Dr. Bak is not ready to stop. As volume one covers 12 months of journey, volume 2 covers 6 months. Well, volume 3 covers 4 months. The speed is building up and increasing, steadily. This is volume 4, RISING, after breaking the sound barrier. Dr. Bak has reached a state where he is above most resistance and friction, he is now in a universe of his own, discovering his powers as he walks his journeys. This is no fiction story or wishful thinking, THE POWER OF YES is the journey of Dr. Bak, from one world record to the next, from one book to the next. You too can walk your own legend, you just need to listen to your innersole and to open up to the opportunity. May you get inspiration from the legendary journey of Dr. Bak and find your own Destiny. Welcome to the Alphas.

THE RISE OF THE UNICORN -038
BY Dr. BAK NGUYEN & Dr. JEAN DE SERRES

In THE RISE OF THE UNICORN, Dr. Bak is joining forces with his friend and mentor, Dr. Jean De Serres. Together both men had many achievements in their respective industries, but the advent of eHappyPedia, THE RISE OF THE UNICORN is a personal project dear to both of them: the QUEST OF HAPPINESS and its empowerment. This book is a special one since you are witnessing the conversation between two entrepreneurs looking to change the world by building unique tools and media. Just like any enterprise, the ride is never a smooth one in the park on a beautiful day. But this is about eHappyPedia, it is about happiness, right? So it will happen and with a smile attached to it! The unique value of this book is that you are sharing the ups and downs of the launch of a Unicorn, not just the glory of the fame, but also the doubts and challenges on the way. May it inspire you on your own journey to success and happiness.

THE RISE OF THE UNICORN 2 -076
eHappyPedia
BY Dr. BAK NGUYEN & Dr. JEAN DE SERRES

This is 2 years after starting the first tome. Dr. Bak's brand is picking up, between the accumulation of records and the recognition. eHappyPedia is now hot for a comeback. In THE RISE OF THE UNICORN 2, Dr. Bak is retracing and addressing each of Dr. Jean De Serres' concerns about the weakness of the first version of eHappyPedia and the eHappy movement. This is the sort of the creation and a UNICORN both in finance and in psychology. Never before, you will assist in such daily and decision-making process of a world phenomenon and of a company. Dr. Bak and Dr. De Serres are literally using the process of writing this series of books to plan and to brainstorm the birth of a bluechip. More than an intriguing story, this is the journey of 2 experienced entrepreneurs changing the world.

THE U.A.X STORY -072
THE ULTIMATE AUDIO EXPERIENCE
BY Dr. BAK NGUYEN

This is the story of the ULTIMATE AUDIO EXPERIENCE, U.A.X. Follow Dr. Bak's footstep on how he invented a new way to read and to learn. Dr. Bak brings his experience as a movie producer and a director to elevate the reading experience to another level with entertaining value and make it accessible to everyone, auditive, and visual people alike.

Three years plus of research and development, countless hours of trials and errors, Dr. Bak finally solved his puzzle: having written more than 1.1 million words. The irony is that he does not like to read, he likes audiobooks! U.A.X. finally allowed the opening of Dr. Bak's entire library to a new genre and media. U.A.X. is the new way to learn and enjoy Audiobooks. Made to be entertaining while keeping the self-educational value of a book, U.A.X. will appeal to both auditive and visual people. U.A.X. is the blockbuster of the Audiobooks. The format has already been approved by iTunes, Amazon, Spotify, and all major platforms for global distribution and streaming.

THE VACCINE -077
BY Dr. BAK NGUYEN & WILLIAM BAK

In THE VACCINE, A TALE OF SPIES AND ALIENS, Dr. Bak reprise his role as mentor to William, his 10 years-old son, both as co-author and as doctor. William is living through the COVID war and has accumulated many, many questions. That morning, they got out all at once. From a conversation between father and son, Dr. Bak is making science into words keeping the interest of his son a Saturday morning in bed. William is not just an audience, he is responsible to map the field with his questions. What started as a morning conversation between father and son, became within the next hour, a great project, their 23rd book together. Learn about the virus, vaccination while entertaining your kids.

TO OVERACHIEVE EVERYTHING BEING LAZY -090
CHEAT YOUR WAY TO SUCCESS
BY Dr. BAK NGUYEN

In TO OVERACHIEVE EVERYTHING BEING LAZY, Dr. Bak retaking his role talking to the millennials, the next generation. If in the first tome of the series LAZY, Dr. Bak addresses the general audience of millennials, especially young women, he is dedicating this tome to the ALPHA amongst the millennials, those aiming for the moon and looking, not only to be happy but to change the world. This is not another take on how to cheat your way to success or how to leverage laziness, but this is the recipe to build overachievers and rainmakers. For the young leaders with ambitions and talent, understanding TIME and ENERGY are crucial from your first steps writing your our legend. If Dr. Bak had the chance to do it all over again, this is how he would do it! Welcome to the Alphas.

TORNADO -067
FORCE OF CHANGE
BY Dr. BAK NGUYEN

In TORNADO - FORCE OF CHANGE Dr. Bak is writing solo. In the midst of the COVID war, change is not a good intention anymore. Change, constant change has become a new reality, a new norm. From somebody who holds the title of Industries' Disruptor, how does he yield change to stay in control? Well, the changes from the COVID war are constant fear and much loss of individual liberty. Some can endure the change, some will ride it. Dr. Bak is sharing his angle of navigating the changes, yielding the improvisations, and to reinvent the goals, the means to stay relevant. From fighting to keep his companies Dr. Bak went on to let go the uncontrollable to embrace the opportunity, he reinvented himself to ride the change and create opportunities from an unprecedented crisis. This is the story of a man refusing to kneel and accept defeat, smiling back at faith to find leverage and hope.

TOUCHSTONE -073
LEVERAGING TODAY'S PSYCHOLOGICAL SMOG
BY Dr. BAK NGUYEN & Dr. KEN SEROTA

TOUCHSTONE, LEVERAGING TODAY'S PSYCHOLOGICAL SMOG is mapping to navigate and to thrive in today's high and constant stress environment. After 40 years in practice, Dr. Serota is concerned about the evolution of the career of health care professionals and the never-ending level of stress. What is stress, what are its effects, damages, and symptoms? If COVID-19 revealed to the world that we are fragile, it also revealed most of the broken and the flaws of our system. For now a century, dentistry has been a champion in depression, Dr.ug addiction, and suicide rate, and the curve is far from flattening. Dr. Bak is sharing his perspective and experience dealing with stress and how to leverage it into a constructive force. From the stress of a doctor with

166

no right to failure to the stress of an entrepreneur never knowing the future, Dr. Bak is sharing his way to use stress as leverage.

From Canada, **Dr BAK NGUYEN**, Nominee Ernst and Young Entrepreneur of the year, Grand Homage Lys DIVERSITY, and LinkedIn & TownHall Achiever of the year. Dr Bak is a cosmetic dentist, CEO and founder of Mdex & Co. His company is revolutionizing the dental field. Speaker and motivator, he wrote 72 books over 36 months accumulating many world records (to be officialized).

- **ENTREPRENEURSHIP**
- **LEADERSHIP**
- **QUEST OF IDENTITY**
- **DENTISTRY AND MEDICINE**
- **PARENTING**
- **CHILDREN BOOKS**
- **PHILOSOPHY**

In 2003, he founded Mdex, a dental company upon which in 2018, he launched the most ambitious private endeavour to reform the dental industry, Canada wide. Philosopher, he has close to his heart the quest of happiness of the people surrounding him, patients and colleagues alike. In 2020, he launched an International collaborative initiative named **THE ALPHAS** to share knowledge and for Entrepreneurs and Doctors to thrive through the Greatest Pandemic and Economic depression of our time.

In 2016, he co-found with Tranie Vo, Emotive World Incorporated, a tech research company to use technology to empower happiness and sharing. U.A.X. the ultimate audio experience is the landmark project on which the team is advancing, utilizing the technics of the movie industry and the advancement in ARTIFICIAL INTELLIGENCE to save the book industry and to upgrade the continuing education space.

These projects have allowed Dr Nguyen to attract interests from the international and diplomatic community and he is now the center of a global discussion in the wellbeing and the future of the health profession. It is in that matter that he shares his thoughts and encourages the health community to share their own stories.

"It's not worth it go through it alone! Together, we stand, alone, we fall."

Motivational speaker and serial entrepreneur, philosopher and author, from his own words, Dr Nguyen describes himself as a dentist by circumstances, an entrepreneur by nature and a communicator by passion.

He also holds recognitions from the Canadian Parliament and the Canadian Senate.

www.DrBakNguyen.com

UAX

ULTIMATE AUDIO EXPERIENCE

A new way to learn and enjoy Audiobooks. Made to be entertaining while keeping the self-educational value of a book, UAX will appeal to both auditive and visual people. UAX is the blockbuster of the Audiobooks.

UAX will cover most of Dr Bak's books, and is now negotiating to bring more authors and more titles to the UAX concept. Now streaming on Spotify, Apple Music and available for download on all major music platforms. Give it a try today!

AMAZON - BARNES & NOBLE - APPLE BOOKS - KINDLE
SPOTIFY - APPLE MUSIC

FROM THE SAME AUTHOR
Dr Bak Nguyen

www.DrBakNguyen.com

MAJOR LEAGUES' ACCESS

FACTEUR HUMAIN -035
LE LEADERSHIP DU SUCCÈS
par Dr. BAK NGUYEN & CHRISTIAN TRUDEAU

THE RISE OF THE UNICORN -038
BY Dr. BAK NGUYEN & Dr. JEAN DE SERRES

CHAMPION MINDSET -039
LEARNING TO WIN
BY Dr. BAK NGUYEN & CHRISTOPHE MULUMBA

THE RISE OF THE UNICORN 2 -076
eHappyPedia
BY Dr. BAK NGUYEN & Dr. JEAN DE SERRES

BRANDING -044
BALANCING STRATEGY AND EMOTIONS
BY Dr. BAK NGUYEN

002 - **La Symphonie des Sens**
ENTREPREUNARIAT
par Dr. BAK NGUYEN

006 - **INDUSTRIES DISRUPTORS**
BY Dr .BAK NGUYEN

007 - **Changing the World
from a dental chair**
BY Dr. BAK NGUYEN

008 - **The Power Behind the Alpha**
BY TRANIE VO & Dr. BAK NGUYEN

036 - **SELFMADE**
GRATITUDE AND HUMILITY
BY Dr. BAK NGUYEN

072 - **THE U.A.X. STORY**
THE ULTIMATE AUDIO EXPERIENCE
BY Dr. BAK NGUYEN

088 - **CRYPTOCONOMICS 101**
MY PERSONAL JOURNEY
FROM 50K TO 1 MILLION
BY Dr BAK NGUYEN

BUSINESS

SYMPHONY OF SKILLS -001
BY Dr. BAK NGUYEN

CHICKEN'S BRAIN
with William Bak

The Trilogy of Legends

THE LEGEND OF THE **CHICKEN HEART** -016
LA LÉGENDE DU **COEUR DE POULET** -017
BY Dr. BAK NGUYEN & WILLIAM BAK

THE LEGEND OF THE **LION HEART** -018
LA LÉGENDE DU **COEUR DE LION** -019
BY Dr. BAK NGUYEN & WILLIAM BAK

THE LEGEND OF THE **DRAGON HEART** -020
LA LÉGENDE DU **COEUR DE DRAGON** -021
BY Dr. BAK NGUYEN & WILLIAM BAK

WE ARE ALL **DRAGONS** -022
NOUS TOUS, **DRAGONS** -023
BY Dr. BAK NGUYEN & WILLIAM BAK

THE **9** SECRETS OF THE **SMART CHICKEN** -025
LES 9 SECRETS DU **POULET INTELLIGENT** -026
BY Dr. BAK NGUYEN & WILLIAM BAK

THE SECRET OF THE **FAST CHICKEN** -027
LE SECRETS DU **POULET RAPIDE** -028
BY Dr. BAK NGUYEN & WILLIAM BAK

THE LEGEND OF THE **SUPER CHICKEN** -029
LA LÉGENDE DU **SUPER POULET** -030
BY Dr. BAK NGUYEN & WILLIAM BAK

031- **THE STORY OF THE CHICKEN SHIT**
032- L'HISTOIRE DU **CACA DE POULET**
BY Dr. BAK NGUYEN & WILLIAM BAK

033- **WHY CHICKEN CAN'T DREAM?**
034- **POURQUOI LES POULETS NE RÊVENT PAS?**
BY Dr. BAK NGUYEN & WILLIAM BAK

057- **THE STORY OF THE CHICKEN NUGGET**
083- **HISTOIRE DE POULET: LA PÉPITE**
BY Dr. BAK NGUYEN & WILLIAM BAK

082- **CHICKEN FOREVER**
084- **POULET POUR TOUJOURS**
BY Dr BAK NGUYEN & WILLIAM BAK

THE SPIES AND ALIENS
COLLECTION

077- **THE VACCINE**
079- **LE VACCIN**
077B- **LA VACUNA**
BY Dr BAK NGUYEN & WILLIAM BAK
TRANSLATION BY BRENDA GARCIA

PROFESSION HEALTH - TOME ONE -005
THE UNCONVENTIONAL
QUEST OF HAPPINESS
BY Dr. BAK NGUYEN, Dr. MIRJANA SINDOLIC,
Dr. ROBERT DURAND AND COLLABORATORS

HOW TO NOT FAIL AS A DENTIST -047
BY Dr. BAK NGUYEN

SUCCESS IS A CHOICE -060
BLUEPRINTS FOR HEALTH
PROFESSIONALS
BY Dr. BAK NGUYEN

RELEVANCY - TOME TWO -064
REINVENTING OURSELVES TO SURVIVE
BY Dr. BAK NGUYEN & Dr. PAUL OUELLETTE AND
COLLABORATORS

MIDAS TOUCH -065
POST-COVID DENTISTRY
BY Dr. BAK NGUYEN, Dr. JULIO REYNAFARJE AND
Dr. PAUL OUELLETTE

THE POWER OF DR -066
THE MODERN TITLE OF NOBILITY
BY Dr. BAK NGUYEN, Dr. PAVEL KRASTEV AND
COLLABORATORS

004- **IDENTITY**
THE ANTHOLOGY OF QUESTS
BY Dr. BAK NGUYEN

011- **HYBRID**
THE MODERN QUEST OF IDENTITY
BY Dr. BAK NGUYEN

045- **HORIZON, BUILDING UP THE VISION**
VOLUME ONE
BY Dr. BAK NGUYEN

048- **HORIZON, ON THE FOOTSTEPS
OF TITANS**
VOLUME TWO
BY Dr. BAK NGUYEN

068- **HORIZON, DREAMING OF TRAVELING**
VOLUME THREE
BY Dr. BAK NGUYEN

062- **RISING**
TO WIN MORE THAN
YOU ARE AFRAID TO LOSE
BY Dr. BAK NGUYEN

067- **TORNADO**
FORCE OF CHANGE
BY Dr. BAK NGUYEN

071- **BOOTCAMP**
BOOKS TO REWRITE MINDSETS
INTO WINNING STATES OF MIND
BY Dr. BAK NGUYEN

078- **POWERPLAY**
HOW TO BUILD THE PERFECT TEAM
BY Dr. BAK NGUYEN

MOMENTUM TRANSFER -009
BY Dr. BAK NGUYEN & Coach DINO MASSON

LEVERAGE -014
COMMUNICATION INTO SUCCESS
BY Dr. BAK NGUYEN AND COLLABORATORS

**HOW TO WRITE A BOOK
IN 30 DAYS** -042
BY Dr. BAK NGUYEN

POWER -043
EMOTIONAL INTELLIGENCE
BY Dr. BAK NGUYEN

**HOW TO WRITE A SUCCESSFUL
BUSINESS PLAN** -049
BY Dr BAK NGUYEN & ROUBA SAKR

MINDSET ARMORY -050
BY Dr. BAK NGUYEN

**MASTERMIND, 7 WAYS INTO THE
BIG LEAGUE** -052
BY Dr. BAK NGUYEN & JONAS DIOP

PLAYBOOK INTRODUCTION -055
BY Dr. BAK NGUYEN

PLAYBOOK INTRODUCTION 2 -056
BY Dr. BAK NGUYEN

024- **THE BOOK OF LEGENDS**
BY Dr. BAK NGUYEN & WILLIAM BAK

041- **THE BOOK OF LEGENDS 2**
BY Dr. BAK NGUYEN & WILLIAM BAK

086- **THE BOOK OF LEGENDS 3**
THE END OF THE INNOCENCE AGE
BY Dr. BAK NGUYEN & WILLIAM BAK

PERSONAL GROWTH

REBOOT -012
MIDLIFE CRISIS
BY Dr. BAK NGUYEN

HUMILITY FOR SUCCESS -051
BALANCING STRATEGY AND EMOTIONS
BY Dr. BAK NGUYEN

THE ENERGY FORMULA -053
BY Dr. BAK NGUYEN

AMONGST THE ALPHA -058
BY Dr. BAK NGUYEN & COACH JONAS DIOP

AMONGST THE ALPHA vol.2 -059
ON THE OTHER SIDE
BY Dr. BAK NGUYEN & COACH JONAS DIOP

THE 90 DAYS CHALLENGE -061
BY Dr. BAK NGUYEN

EMPOWERMENT -069
BY Dr BAK NGUYEN

THE MODERN WOMAN -070
TO HAVE IT HAVE WITH NO SACRIFICE
BY Dr. BAK NGUYEN & Dr. EMILY LETRAN

ALPHA LADDERS -075
CAPTAIN OF YOUR DESTINY
BY Dr BAK NGUYEN & JONAS DIOP

080- **1SELF**
REINVENT YOURSELF
FROM ANY CRISIS
BY Dr BAK NGUYEN

THE LAZY FRANCHISE

089- **THE CONFESSION OF
A LAZY OVERACHIEVER**
BY Dr BAK NGUYEN

090- **TO OVERACHIEVE
EVERYTHING BEING LAZY**
CHEAT YOUR WAY TO SUCCESS
BY Dr BAK NGUYEN

PHILOSOPHY

003- **LEADERSHIP** -003
PANDORA'S BOX
BY Dr. BAK NGUYEN

015- **FORCES OF NATURE**
FORGING THE CHARACTER
OF WINNERS
BY Dr BAK NGUYEN

040- **KRYPTO**
TO SAVE THE WORLD
BY Dr. BAK NGUYEN & ILYAS BAKOUCH

ALPHA LADDERS 2 - 081
SHAPING LEADERS AND ACHIEVERS
BY Dr BAK NGUYEN & BRENDA GARCIA

MIRROR - 085
BY Dr BAK NGUYEN

099 - **306 HAPPINESS QUOTES**
SHORTCUT VOLUME SEVEN
BY Dr. BAK NGUYEN

100 - **170 DOCTOR QUOTES**
SHORTCUT VOLUME EIGHT
BY Dr. BAK NGUYEN

408 HEALING QUOTES - 093
SHORTCUT VOLUME ONE
BY Dr. BAK NGUYEN

408 GROWTH QUOTES - 094
SHORTCUT VOLUME TWO
BY Dr. BAK NGUYEN

365 LEADERSHIP QUOTES - 095
SHORTCUT VOLUME THREE
BY Dr. BAK NGUYEN

518 CONFIDENCE QUOTES - 096
SHORTCUT VOLUME FOUR
BY Dr. BAK NGUYEN

317 SUCCESS QUOTES - 097
SHORTCUT VOLUME FIVE
BY Dr. BAK NGUYEN

376 POWER QUOTES - 098
SHORTCUT VOLUME SIX
BY Dr. BAK NGUYEN

013 - **LE RÊVE CANADIEN**
D'IMMIGRANT À MILLIONNAIRE
par DR BAK NGUYEN

054 - **CHOC**
LE JARDIN D'EDITH
par DR BAK NGUYEN

063 - **AFTERMATH**
BUSINESS AFTER THE GREAT PAUSE
BY Dr BAK NGUYEN & Dr ERIC LACOSTE

073 - **TOUCHSTONE**
LEVERAGING TODAY'S
PSYCHOLOGICAL SMOG
BY Dr BAK NGUYEN & Dr KEN SEROTA

074 - **COVIDCONOMICS**
THE GENERATION AHEAD
BY Dr BAK NGUYEN

THE POWER OF YES

046 - **THE POWER OF YES 3**
VOLUME THREE: LIMITLESS
BY Dr BAK NGUYEN

087 - **THE POWER OF YES 4**
VOLUME FOUR: PURPOSE
BY Dr BAK NGUYEN

THE POWER OF YES - 010
VOLUME ONE: IMPACT
BY Dr BAK NGUYEN

091 - **THE POWER OF YES 5**
VOLUME FIVE: ALPHA
BY Dr BAK NGUYEN

THE POWER OF YES 2 - 037
VOLUME TWO: SHAPELESS
BY Dr BAK NGUYEN

092 - **THE POWER OF YES 6**
VOLUME SIX: PERSPECTIVE
BY Dr BAK NGUYEN

www.DrBakNguyen.com

AMAZON - BARNES & NOBLE - APPLE BOOKS - KINDLE
SPOTIFY - APPLE MUSIC

DR.

Bak Nguyen

www.ingramcontent.com/pod-product-compliance
Lightning Source LLC
Chambersburg PA
CBHW060752050426
42449CB00008B/1373